Praise for Being Fruitful Without Multiplying

"As the Founder of Gateway Women, an organisation for women who are childless by circumstance, I recognise the authenticity of the voices in *Being Fruitful Without Multiplying*. Public discourse around 'why' women don't have children falls into two very simplistic categories: either the women couldn't have them or they didn't want them. *Being Fruitful Without Multiplying* explodes this reductive view by giving voice to the many different ways that a woman finds herself without children. From choice, circumstance, medical, religious, cultural and societal factors, each woman shares her story of how she has navigated the assumptions and expectations of her family and culture as a woman without children. The latter half of the book, featuring 'first person' narratives from women of all ages and backgrounds, brings into printed form what is normally only seen in the safety of anonymous childfree Internet forums, and may serve to broaden the simplistic assumptions that are often made about 'why' or 'how' women remain childless. This book is destined to become a valuable social document for researchers, as well as a friend to culturally and socially isolated childless by choice women. *Being Fruitful Without Multiplying* is an important work, and I commend the authors for their efforts and honesty in sharing their own stories in such depth, as well as collating so many other voices from around the globe."

—Jody Day, Founder, Gateway Women, UK

"Patricia Yvette, Renee Ann, and Janice Lynne have opened their journals and have collaborated to bring us a thoughtful and insightful collection of stories and essays allowing us to explore the diverse lives and experiences of childfree women and men from around the world. The essays featured in *Being Fruitful Without Multiplying* reflect what I found to be some of the top motives for choosing and embracing a life without biological children—freedom, independence, and quality-of-life—and they serve to validate the experiences and feelings of all who have challenged the assumption of parenthood. I would recommend this book to anyone who has made this choice or is currently childless and wonders 'What can I expect if I remain so?' "

—Laura S. Scott, Author of *Two Is Enough: A Couple's Guide to Living Childless by Choice* and Director of the Childless by Choice Project.

"*Being Fruitful Without Multiplying* is an easy-reading book offering stories from the lives of three women, and vignettes from those of many others, about the important topic of women choosing to be 'childless' or 'childfree.' The book discusses numerous reasons why so many women these days make this choice, including financial considerations, lack of maternal desire, fear of pregnancy, concern over body image changes, career priorities, childhood influences, and numerous psychological explanations. The fact is that all human behavior makes sense if only one understands the dynamics that drive and shape it. Sometimes those forces are consciously understood and sometimes they are just below the surface, waiting to be revealed. Each of the primary stories in this book, and many of the others, address forces that ultimately have a psychological origin, whether they realize it or not. Also presented is the array of mixed messages childless women receive from their families and society around the decision not to bear children. This holds true across numerous nations and cultures irrespective of the social progress many women have made in their ability to make such personal decisions. Then of course there is also the matter of contributing to the rearing of children without giving them birth, a topic less focally addressed in this book but increasingly more significant as ever more women feel free to go childless. This is a book that will be interesting to all women and the men who strive to understand them."

—Glenn Ross Caddy Ph.D. A.B.P.P., F.A.P.A., Clinical Director, Mind-Experts International, Fort Lauderdale, Florida

"*Being Fruitful Without Multiplying* adds an important voice to the ongoing discussions regarding women's reproductive choices. The authors have impressively gathered stories from women around the world of all age groups who each share their own intimate reasons for choosing not to procreate. The collection celebrates the opportunities its contributors have gained from their decisions and illustrates the many affirming roles that children can nevertheless play in their lives. This is a terrific resource for expanding our perspectives on parenting, reproduction and the shifting economic and social realities in women's lives. I recommend it to academic and nonacademic audiences alike."

—Maythee Rojas, Ph.D., Associate Professor of Women's Gender & Sexuality Studies at California State University, Long Beach

"As someone who struggles deeply with the question of whether or not to have a baby, I found this book to be an insightful and inspiring resource. I quite simply couldn't put it down! Breaking the entries down by age group was so interesting, because it allowed me to see the progression of how people felt about their decision from their twenties all the way into their fifties. .... But the ones I found most interesting were those that gave me new insights into understanding why I have always felt so different from other women my age who have always known they wanted a baby. .... If you're looking for insights, trying to decide to have a baby, or have already decided to go Childfree and are just looking for validation or to hear from those who share your experiences, this book is an excellent source of support!"

—Liz Ference, MaybeBabyMaybeNot.com

"As a practicing Clinical Mental Health Counselor, I feel that the personal short stories in this book will help countless individuals who have decided not to have children. Many of my clients come into my office with their presenting issue that they have decided not to have children and want to know what is wrong with them. I explain to them that not all people decide to have children for various reasons and there is nothing wrong with their decision."

—Adam Colando, Clinical Mental Health Counselor

"It's important for people to realize that life, purpose and God's design and plan do go on for those who do not procreate. I believe it is THE plan for a few, as *Being Fruitful Without Multiplying* so eloquently illustrates, not as a result of what didn't happen in life, but rather a decision for fullness of purpose and the fulfillment of a plan. 'And we know that all things work together for good to those who love God, to those who are the called according to His purpose. For whom He foreknew, He also predestined ....' Rom. 8:28-30 NKJV."

—Dr. Lyrica Joy, Bishop and Founder, The International Church for ALL Nations

Being Fruitful Without Multiplying

Being Fruitful Without Multiplying

Stories and Essays from around the World

Patricia Yvette

Renee Ann

Janice Lynne

and Many Others

coffeetownpress

Seattle, WA

coffeetownpress

Coffeetown Press
PO Box 70515
Seattle, WA 98127

For more information contact: www.coffeetownpress.com

Cover design by Sabrina Sun

Being Fruitful Without Multiplying
Copyright © 2013 by Patricia Yvette

ISBN: 978-1-60381-155-2 (Trade Paperback)
ISBN: 978-1-60381-156-9 (eBook)

LOC Control Number: 2012941558

Printed in the United States of America

www.BeingFruitfulWithoutMultiplying.com

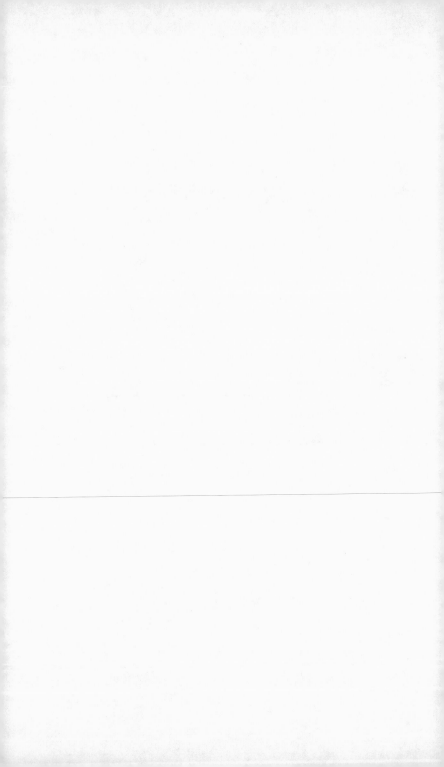

To my two co-authors and all the contributors:
Without your candid contributions this book would not be possible.

To Eric, my husband and best friend:
May the love, laughter and adventure never end.

To Coco and Kenya:
Whose unconditional love brings great joy to our lives.

In Loving memory of my mother, Eva:
Who loved and sacrificed for her family.

To my father, Ricardo:
Who is full of optimism, humor, and wisdom; you are an inspiration.

To Richard, Karla and their kids, Richie and Zak:
Never a dull moment.

To my good friend Mike Lettini for recommending Coffeetown Press; and to Coffeetown Press for giving this book a chance.

To our editor, Catherine Treadgold, for her dedicated hard work editing and shaping this book.

And finally, to all the Childfree and Childless, and those deciding whether or not to bear children:
You are not alone.

Contents

Stories and Essays from around the World

Twenties

Thirties

"Go Confidently in the Direction of Your Dreams,
Live the Life you've imagined ..."

—Henry David Thoreau.

Introduction

It happened in Seattle, on a cool winter evening during a cooking class at our instructor's home overlooking Lake Washington. We had just finished cooking our first meal featuring New Orleans cuisine and were serving ourselves such delicacies as shrimp Arnaud, chicken okra gumbo, snap bean salad, beignets, and bananas Foster.

I sat near an open window, away from the overheated and overcrowded kitchen. It was raining and the cool breeze was refreshing after all the hours spent cooking. A classmate walked over and sat on the couch across from me.

After a few minutes of conversation about the class and the recipes, she asked, "Do you have any children?"

It is not unusual for this topic—personal as it is—to come up in small talk with new acquaintances. Feeling much too relaxed to delve into the reasoning behind my decision not to have children, I simply said "No" and smiled as I enjoyed my spicy chicken gumbo.

Smiling back, she said, "I didn't think so. You look too together to have kids."

Her response startled me. Typically, my answer would earn a long stare, followed by an immediate change of subject or the intrusive question, "Why?"

It took me a few moments, but I finally responded with, "Thanks, how about you?"

Nodding her head once, she said, "I have five boys. My husband gave me a gift certificate for this cooking class. It's the first night out I've had in a long time."

That evening was the first time somebody I did not know personally had responded respectfully and matter-of-factly when I acknowledged I did not have children. Normally this was a subject I preferred to avoid. Let's face it, even today it is considered a bit out of the ordinary not to have children. "Childless" couples are typically pitied or considered selfish or somehow deficient. After all, "First comes love, then comes marriage, then comes baby in a baby carriage," right?

That evening was the moment of conception for this book, setting off a thought process that led me to examine my choice in depth. I suppose all people do retrospectives at various stages of their lives, and the age of forty was a milestone for me. However, after that night, exploring the reasons behind my decision not to reproduce became a priority. I had consciously taken the road less traveled, and while I knew some of the reasons, I yearned to explore them in more depth.

I had become so accustomed to my fast-paced lifestyle that initially, my mission was difficult. I began to shift gears, slow down a bit, set aside time to reflect. I started a journal, jotting down memorable experiences that might have contributed to my decision. The more memories I documented, the more questions arose. I recalled pivotal moments—both positive and negative—in my youth.

I was intrigued to discover what a dramatic impression many of my childhood experiences had made on me. Couples with children have no idea how ostracized couples who have no children—for whatever reason— can feel. In time I realized it would be a cop-out to bear children simply to satisfy society's expectations.

Eventually I discovered not only an answer to my question, "Why did I choose not to bear children?" but was able to track the experiences that led me to my present lifestyle. I was so surprised by these insights that I invited two of my relatives to embark on the same journey. And so, *Being Fruitful without Multiplying* was born.

Our initial intention in writing this book was to provide a look into the lives of three women—each a decade apart. Renee and Janice joined me in this process because we had so much in common. We all wanted to explore the world, expand our horizons intellectually, excel as career women, and find more ways to express ourselves creatively. The stories provided by Renee and Janice made me wonder about what other factors might contribute to a decision not to bear children.

Our collaboration expanded my original goals. Thanks to the

Internet, our reach extended beyond the Seattle area to the entire nation, and eventually throughout the world. We were able to connect with women (and a few men) from different countries, cultures and income groups who were willing to share their personal narratives and childhood reflections.

While researching this book, we discovered many virtual societies, both private and open forums, dedicated to the "Childfree." This new word "Childfree" was coined as a reaction to the negative connotations of the word "childless." When people refer to me as childless, I feel their pity. "Childfree" implies I had a choice.

The word "Childfree" is used quite often by our contributors. Although this book concentrates mainly on a lifestyle that does not include reproducing biologically, it does not rule out raising children—taking care of the world's children, including those from your spouse's first marriage.

We were fascinated by all the essays that came in. So many more reasons for not bearing children existed than we anticipated.

The American Dream, Revisited

American women have made enormous progress legally since our "forefathers" drafted the constitution. We are equal under the law: we can vote, sue, write our own wills, sit on juries, etc. Although many would argue we still don't receive equal pay for equal work, we are slowly making headway. Where we seem to be taking a step backward is in reproductive rights. There is a certain vocal faction who believe women should not be given easy access to abortion, even early-term, and that insurance should not cover birth control.

Women have definitely made progress when it comes to deciding our own lifestyles. The Internet has made an enormous difference to a particular group of women who used to feel totally isolated—those who have chosen not to reproduce.

In *Being Fruitful Without Multiplying,* we set out to give voice to individuals everywhere who have chosen not to bear children. All of our contributors were influenced by at least one of the following factors: societal pressure, biological and psychological issues, childhood influences, and economic limitations.

What is considered a normal lifestyle these days? Does the American dream still require success in our chosen field, a loving spouse, a white picket fence, and children? Perhaps we have come to realize that it is not impossible to obtain all of these blessings; we don't have enough time, money, or energy. For some of us, three out of four—even two out of four—ain't bad. Happiness comes in many forms.

Societal Pressure

Most parents urge their children to "carry on the family name" and many friends with children urge their "childless" peers to follow suit so that everyone will continue to share common ground. Society itself applauds motherhood as the "natural" way to go. Children will give you comfort in your old age—or so the conventional wisdom goes.

We used to think we had until menopause to reproduce; now we know that by age thirty our eggs are already starting to deteriorate. If we wait until age forty, our chances of getting pregnant without fertility treatments are just about nil. If we do get pregnant at that late date, we risk having a defective child. The symbol of the ticking clock is so prevalent we can practically hear it resounding in our ears. For those whose careers have been a disappointment, having a baby may seem like a means of accomplishing *something*—at the very least, making your parents happy. Maybe your child can succeed where you failed.

For teenagers—thanks to the media and our celebrity-worshipping culture—having a baby seems like a grand adventure, the way to obtain a real live doll who will love you unconditionally. Sexually naive youngsters fixated on Hollywood "baby mamas" with unlimited funds continue to fall into the single mother trap. It doesn't help that many adults seem determined to limit their birth control options to abstinence.

Many women still believe that having a man's baby is a way to bind him to you forever.

Despite this pressure, more and more young women are reprioritizing their lives and establishing long-term goals beyond motherhood. If the desire to reproduce is there, fine, but why not postpone this desire until you can establish a certain level of self-sufficiency?

Biological and Psychological Issues

Many of our contributors knew from early childhood on that they had no interest in bearing children. They didn't play with baby dolls and they had no desire to "play house." They are certain they were born without the mother instinct. Some women fear or have an aversion to pregnancy and childbirth. Others freely admit that they are too vain; they didn't want their bodies ruined by pregnancy.

Some women could not conceive initially but were later glad of that fact, or chose not to conceive because they carried genetic diseases.

Though not wishing to bear children themselves, many of our contributors have adopted children or cared for stepchildren. They are also enthusiastic aunts, teachers, coaches, and child therapists; they like children but have no desire or need to have their own.

Childhood Influences

Some contributors had their fill of motherhood by the time they themselves came of age. They were either the eldest in large families where their mothers expected them to raise their siblings, or they made a few extra bucks by babysitting the neighbors' unruly offspring. They had already "been there, done that." Others were scared off by their parents' unhappy marriages or by observing unhappy mothers.

Some were afraid of taking on the extra "burden"—after being raised to feel like burdens themselves.

Economic Limitations

In 2009, *Time Magazine's* Nancy Gibbs estimated that it costs parents an average of $221,000 to raise a child to age seventeen. According to www.ParentDish.com, this amount increased to $226,920 in 2011.

No matter how you look at it, raising children is expensive.

Many of our contributors had struggled too much in their childhoods as their parents sought to eke out a living and put bread on the table. They didn't wish to inflict economic hardship on another generation. They were also done with "doing without" themselves. A few women in countries like Russia stated that they simply could not afford children—despite being in professions requiring advanced education.

Women are marrying much later than they used to and often postponing childbirth until they are in their early thirties. More women are taking the time to complete their education before starting families. The more educated a woman is, the longer she may choose to wait—or she may simply decide not to have children at all.

Mothers, especially those with expensive educations, struggle with the question of whether to continue working even though they don't require the income to survive. Just last year Coffeetown Press published an anthology (*Torn: True Stories of Kids, Career & the Conflict of Modern Motherhood*) in which thirty-seven women eloquently share their own struggles to balance work and motherhood. Although they express varying degrees of satisfaction with their choices, there is one matter they all agree upon: you can't "have it all."

The lack of affordable childcare and flexible schedules mean that many college-educated women who become mothers end up in the same position as teen moms: locked into limited career paths that ensure they will never make the same money as their male counterparts and will therefore have a limited voice in business and public policy creation.

The glass ceiling is still a concern. About fifty percent of middle managers are women, but very few are chief executives—about three percent. Many careers are still "mommy tracked," and if these women get divorced, they often have trouble caring for their families.

No wonder the "Childfree" movement is taking off!

America is not the only country where women are choosing to have fewer children, postponing motherhood, or passing on the experience altogether.

Take Brazil ... *National Geographic* (Sept. 2011) featured an article by C. Gorney about how much the Brazilian fertility rate has dropped—to the point where the population is no longer replacing itself. The number of children a woman bears on average is decreasing worldwide; however, it is the speed of Brazil's drop that intrigues demographers. Increased education for girls is a factor, as elsewhere, but in Brazil, the spread of electricity is said to contribute, as is the popularity of evening soap operas called novellas, where women have small families. Because they are having fewer children, more Brazilian women can join the workforce.

They have an expression: "A fábrica está fechada." (The factory is closed.)

Our Contributors and Our Readers

We are grateful to our generous contributors, who were willing to reveal the intimate details of their private lives. My two relatives and I were comforted by hearing the stories of others who share our views and circumstances. We hope others will be comforted as well. And perhaps there are still more readers out there—mothers and fathers by choice—who are curious to know what motivates the rest of us.

Society teaches us that women who do not bear children will never feel complete. This is true for many women. There are others, however, who are not suited to motherhood, whose happiness is found through other forms of creativity. This book gives them a chance to be heard.

Our Personal Memoirs: Establishing Identity and Independence

In the first three stories, Renee, Janice, and I describe pivotal moments in our lives that we felt contributed to our desire to be psychologically and financially independent as well as the impact of societal pressure, relationships, religion and loss, the importance of travel and animals and the role of children.

Stories and Essays from around the World

In this section everyday women, as well as a few men, share the circumstances that led to their being Childfree or Childless. Ranging in age from twenty to sixty-one, they represent seventeen states and thirteen countries outside the U.S.

Author / Editor Discussion

After Renee, Janice and I had read all the stories and essays in this book, we met with our editor, Catherine Treadgold, for a lighthearted lunch. We had collaborated via social networking and email over the course of a year and so welcomed the opportunity to meet in person to discuss everything we had learned from our contributors and one another. If you would like to join in the discussion or have questions for our authors or contributors, feel free to join our Being Fruitful without Multiplying Facebook Group.

Being Fruitful Without Multiplying

The three of us do not claim any particular expertise when it comes to women's issues. What this book offers are honest, heartfelt insights provided by people whose lives have not centered on the fruits of their wombs but on the fruits of their labor and imaginations. We hope that women who have chosen to bear children take no offense. Their sacrifices and joys are celebrated by every culture. We would never presume to sit in judgment of their choices or lifestyles. All we ask is that they respect our choices as well.

And we are simply thrilled to have this opportunity to tell our own stories.

Patricia Yvette's Journal

The Early Years

Ever since I was a little girl, I have had a big imagination. After evening supper and right before sunset, I often indulged in my active routine: swinging from a swing tied to a huge oak tree large enough to occupy most of our backyard in Del Rio, Texas. While my squeaky swing reached higher and higher, I observed the sun slowly descending beyond the horizon and allowed my imagination to roam.

I was a shy little girl who enjoyed playing alone with my Barbie Dolls and stuffed animals, but I was also quite the tomboy who enjoyed the excitement of competition. It took me quite a few years to outgrow the tomboy stage. Outwardly passive, I was nevertheless undaunted by fearful situations. Darkness, full moons, scary movies, basically anything associated with fear excited me—a craving I have not outgrown.

Old black and white Boris Karloff movies still thrill me. Mysterious creatures like Frankenstein, Dracula, King Kong, Godzilla, and the ever-popular humans who morphed into werewolves at the rise of the full moon. Today's horror films disappoint by resorting to violence in order to achieve a minimally frightening affect—or perhaps I have simply built up a tolerance to them over time. Watching scary movies together was a pleasure my father and I shared in my youth. My big brother never seemed as interested, though we do share other traits. His nature was also quiet, although he seldom passed up an opportunity to tease his little sister. We were constantly battling, although all in good fun. Considering our similar upbringing, I am amazed that we have chosen to live our adult lives so differently, that our passions are so opposed.

My brother resides in a small town with his wife and kids, owns his own business, and enjoys spending time at the track, where he either participates in racing events or hangs out with his buddies and sons. He truly enjoys living the small town life. On the other hand, I am drawn to the excitement of a large metropolitan city, with theaters, art museums, jazz clubs, major league sports, and a multitude of fine restaurants. Having the freedom to explore the world is more to my liking than a house filled with children. In spite of our differences, we still share a quiet closeness. As military brats, we tended to be introverted, perhaps because we never knew what the next move would bring.

From the time I was born—the daughter of a hometown beauty queen from Del Rio, Texas, and a high ranking Sergeant in the Air Force— we relocated every two years or so to various places around the world. The greater part of our time was spent between Europe, the Pacific Islands, and the United States. In between moves, we visited Switzerland, Holland, Austria, Luxembourg, Belgium, Japan, the Philippines, and Mexico. It was a whirlwind of a childhood.

Among all the destinations I have visited, the place that remains with me most is the small Pacific Island of Taiwan, also known as Formosa, where we resided for three years.

Wanderlust

As I organized my personal effects, preparing for our next move, I pondered the sad fact that I might never see my friends in Utah again. Even though I had been a veteran of relocating even before my teenage years, the pain associated with our next departure was hard to accept.

We flew in a 747 from Seattle to Hawaii, then to the Philippines and on to Taipei, Taiwan. From Taiwan my mother used the "Mayo Quanchi" flight, a free courier aircraft belonging to the Taiwanese Air Force and made available to Air Force wives and Taiwanese airmen to go on shopping trips to other cities. The rest of us took a cargo plane to our next destination. We spent an uncomfortable, turbulent flight strapped to bench-like seats like parachute jumpers preparing for their next leap. Touching down on the Tainan, Taiwan airport runway didn't improve my mood any.

The mystifying world right outside the cargo door made my stomach flutter as we began to disembark the aircraft. The humidity was so thick it felt like stepping into a steam room. An unusual scent lingered, not bad, not good, but foreign in some way. As we entered the airport, I observed stoned-faced airport security scattered throughout the building. The sound of overlapping foreign languages heightened my sense of confusion. At the time, I didn't realize that what I was actually experiencing was culture shock.

The taxi ride from the airport to the Oriental Hotel was another eye opener. The infrastructure was crammed with taxis, buses, trucks, mopeds, bicycles, and small cars, with no real sign of lanes to guide the congestion. Horns echoed through the air as our taxi driver frantically waved his arm out the window, attempting to merge in front of another car. A bicycle crossed our path, balancing a family of four. Stray animals—dogs, cats, and miniature pigs—wandered the streets freely; I cringed at the thought of one

13

of them getting caught under our wheels. I later discovered that this chaotic traffic mess was just part of our new way of life.

After safely arriving at the Oriental Hotel, we checked into a high-rise suite overlooking the city. This would be our home until the next single-family military housing became available. While my parents and my brother began unpacking and acquainting themselves with our temporary living quarters, I grabbed my father's binoculars from his suitcase. Timidly, I walked to the hotel window, nestled myself behind the two large drapes, and focused in on this unfamiliar world. Old buildings lined the crowded streets, extending out beyond my focus, and the main street in front of our hotel was lined with a kaleidoscope of night market stands; Taiwan's version of a farmer's market. Tourists pawed through jewelry, clothing, and carved wooden statues. The locals shopped for their evening supper, selecting items such as octopus, monkey heads, chicken feet, eels, and an array of assorted freshly caught seafood—none of which bore any similarity to my favorite dishes of macaroni and cheese, pizza, and burgers.

Farther down the road I observed a school bus filled with local kids unloading near the night market stands. The school girls had identical haircuts—short, straight, and just below their ears. All wore beige uniforms, which strikingly resembled Girl Scouts'. The boys wore similar uniforms, except with pants, and all had identical crew cuts. I suddenly imagined myself being forced to wear that uniform and cut my waist-length hair. The strange feeling of culture shock overwhelmed me, and I began to weep.

I went to bed early that evening feeling cold and alone in a very hot and crowded place. Three years later I would be experiencing these same feelings of sadness as we left to return to America.

The following morning was my first day at school, and I was exhausted from the night before. Waiting by the school bus, I spotted another military brat. When she noticed me, she immediately walked over to introduce herself as Gina. She was a southern girl with long blond hair and a welcoming smile. She and I would go on to become lifelong friends. In the military, breaking the ice is easy. With one simple question, "Where are you from?" the rest follows. That was the first of many friendships I would develop in Taiwan. I remain in touch with several of these friends, thanks to the wonderful invention of social networking.

There was only one American school in Tainan, with grade levels ranging from first through senior year. These days that type of school dynamic is practically unheard of in America. Although the school was very small, establishing a variety of relationships between different cliques was possible. The crowds I was drawn to ranged from ages ten to sixteen. All the new social contacts soon snapped me out of my culture shock.

Not only was this school populated with a variety of ages, but also an assortment of ethnic groups. Never had I witnessed such diversity in one school. What astounded me most was the absence of prejudice. This community of kids living in an exotic country and attending the same tiny school embraced one another as simply Americans. The only segregation that existed was the athletic rivalry between the American and Taiwanese schools.

A few months had passed when we finally received word that military housing was available just a short distance from the Air Force base. I loved the exotic environment. Next to our front patio sat a large banana tree loaded with bunches of small green tropical bananas. Scattered around our yard were a variety of interesting insects such as praying mantises with their cute little triangle-shaped heads and tiny lizards quickly darting away at any sudden movement. At first they frightened me, but I later began to enjoy the unusual way they skittered around.

As we settled into our new place, Mother's signature interior design made it feel like "our home." A few modern essentials were lacking, however.

Back then, living in a foreign country gave you the experience of making do with minimal technology. The only American programs available at the time were a three-hour cluster of designated TV shows on one station, including *Burt's Law* and *Starsky & Hutch*. We quickly lost our dependency on television for home entertainment. Radio was a nice alternative entertainment for military brats. *Casey Kasem's American Top 40* was a popular Sunday night ritual.

A strong social bond existed between the American kids in Tainan. The Air Force base had a variety of great gathering spots to choose from—a swimming pool, bowling alley, youth center, movie theaters, an arcade with a pool table, ping pong table, and pinball machines.

The military kids all owned bikes, and the Air Force base was adjacent to our military housing complex, so there was no need to depend on parents for transportation. The older kids looked after the young ones, and we were granted plenty of freedom.

Tainan, Taiwan was considered a relatively safe place to live, and crime was extremely low. At the time, Taiwan was under martial law, and the whole island had been placed under military jurisdiction. The Taiwanese military, mostly Chinese Nationals, made it against the law for civilians to own guns, hold demonstrations, or even grow their hair long. That explained the short haircuts. Because of these restrictions, military parents felt comfortable allowing their kids to wander.

On occasion we were permitted to ride the local bus downtown to hang out or shop. The stationery and candy stores were my favorites. Their plum candy—nicknamed sour balls—was completely addictive. Shaped like Boston Baked Beans, they were grainy in texture and wrinkly like raisins. The orangey rust coating was so sweet and sour my saliva glands would lose all control. Once dissolved, all that remained was the sweet chewy plum inside. The stationery stores carried an assortment of notepad booklets and designer erasers. I still have a few in my possession.

My family collected wooden hand-carved statues, vases, jade and other gem stones. We even had teakwood furniture designed per our specifications, at a much reduced cost than you would find in the United States. Of course I couldn't depart the island without owning two specially designed pairs of jeans and a denim jacket embroidered with brightly colored dragons. I had arrived at the age when appearance was important. My tom boy stage was nearing its end, and a new distraction was coming to the forefront—boys.

During the latter part of my stay in Taiwan I began to long for boys to see me as someone other than their next bike or footrace challenger. Taiwan was the first place where I experienced love, even if it was only puppy love. To my mind, innocent love counts, too.

After living in Tainan, Taiwan, for a few months, I began to notice the diversity this beautiful island had to offer. The endless rice fields were surrounded by mountains, the Chinese art and architecture displayed a story of the history of Taiwan. The calligraphy, paintings, signs, wooden and stone carvings, clay sculptures, and ceramics were all mesmerizing. My favorite attractions were the elegant gold-plated temples. Each entrance displayed a signature statue of a very large, happy golden Buddha.

There were many celebrations and festivals throughout the year, and the streets would be filled with flowing dragons and locals in character costumes with painted faces—all dancing to the unique sounds of Asian music. The festival finale would conclude with a breathtaking display of fireworks that could be witnessed from miles away.

There was positive energy and a sense of unity amongst the Americans in this foreign land. Having the freedom to explore such an exotic place freely and establish such a wealth of friendships left a major impression on such a young girl. The experience planted a seed of wanderlust within my soul that has since blossomed into a desire to discover new cultures and seek out new adventures all over the world.

A Lasting Impression in Asia

One evening I was shopping the Night Markets for a unique jade ring, and I noticed an elderly woman with a patch over one eye sitting on the ground holding a naked baby in her arms, while her weathered hand mixed a basket of what appeared to be gemstones. Beside her was a small child wearing a dirty dress, no shoes and playing with a wooden flute. The woman looked up at me and held out her palm, displaying an assortment of brilliantly colored stones; a shiny gold tooth stood out between her smiling lips.

This scene reminded me of the time our family visited Tijuana, Mexico. While my family and I walked downtown, shopping for souvenirs, a young woman approached us offering us her infant to hold. At least, it appeared that she wanted my mother simply to hold her child. Then she began to speak Spanish to my parents, and they quickly guided my brother and me in the opposite direction. I asked my parents, "What did she want?" No response. Then it occurred to me, the woman was trying to give my mother her child … permanently. My father explained her hardships to me, that she simply wanted a better life for her child.

Observing the foreign little girl at the Night Market made me wonder what had happened to that baby in Mexico. Had she been given away, or did she now resemble the child standing before me. Was she even still alive? Although a child myself, I never forgot that encounter; it was a defining moment in my life.

Residing in other countries helped form my vision of the world. There appeared to be a lot of need but not enough sacrifice. It was during this time that I began to question whether I ever wanted to have my own children when so many were living in adverse conditions. My peers, in contrast, shared a different perspective.

One day after school, I met with some girlfriends at the local youth center and the subject of babies arose. The majority of the girls were enthusiastic about the prospect of having their own babies. "Babies are so cute and fun!" I recall one girl saying. I sat there quietly listening to their reasoning, unable to relate. Yes, babies are adorable, and kids can be a lot of fun, but why not adopt instead?

The conversation seemed to center on having a child that resembled oneself—a "mini-me." I wondered if perhaps I would one day adopt one of those deprived children instead of bearing my own. It was a question that would haunt me for the next twenty years.

The Bear Trap

The faces awaiting me at the school bus stop in our next destination were nowhere near as welcoming as those in Taiwan.

Following our three years in Asia, we departed the warm humid climate for the freezing cold temperatures of the Upper Peninsula of Michigan. Transitioning into this new school dynamic was as difficult as adapting to the change in temperature.

As the door to the school bus swung open that first morning, a gruff-looking older man—with absolutely no glimmer of kindness—stared at me, still holding onto the door lever, as if he would close it at any moment if I didn't step in immediately. I didn't know what to think of the small bat leaning next to the stick shift.

Stepping onto the bus, I turned to face the other students, sitting scrunched together, three in each seat, occupying the first six or seven rows. As I started to take the next available seat by the window, all the students shouted in unison, "You can't sit there!" Surprised by the outburst, I turned and glanced at the bus driver for direction, but he just stared at me through the rearview mirror with his big bloodshot blue eyes, waiting for my next move. Finally, two of the girls slid over hesitantly and offered me a seat.

The small town of Gwinn, Michigan was one tough community. As I discovered, watching their backs during lunch break was a skill new students learned quickly. Although I drew glances from many of the boys (who looked much older than those at my previous school), the girls were the ones who concerned me. Cliques had already been established the previous year and new students were given a hard time, especially the minorities and military brats. Bullying was a major problem; fortunately, I had acquired martial arts training from a Master Kung Fu Artist in Tainan, Taiwan, and my skills in defense came in handy. The bus would drop us off at our school, but would pick us up off school grounds, which required a daily walk through a heavily wooded trail. After school the tough guys and gals would hang in the woods, smoking cigarettes or marijuana. I encountered more than my fair share of fights during my hikes through the woods. It was either fight or not defend myself at all, and that's just not who I am.

Eventually, I eased my way up the social ladder, fitting into many different cliques, which I preferred anyway; no one clique retained my interest for long. Unfortunately, it wasn't too long after I had finally found a way to fit in that my father made an announcement: after twenty years in the Air Force, he felt it was the right time to retire and settle down.

The following summer we packed up our motor home for a road trip to Idaho. We drew our trip out by several weeks, turning this last move into an adventure by visiting several National Parks along the way.

Destination Idaho threw me for a loop. After a few weeks living there a familiar feeling settled in: culture shock—or rather, lack-of-culture shock. Furthermore, we were no longer considered "military," but "civilians." I soon realized we had reached the end of our journey. No more moving, no more saying goodbye to friends, and no more new discoveries in foreign lands. It was a bitter-sweet transition.

Following high school, I lacked direction, so after only two semesters at the local university I dropped out. Finding a steady job with a decent income was next on my agenda.

From ages twelve to eighteen, I earned the majority of my income babysitting. I'm not sure why, but kids really seemed to like having me around. Kids would request me as their babysitter over other sitters. One summer I even worked as a nine-to-five nanny for two young girls still in diapers—now *that* was an eye-opener into the challenges of child care!

Those six years of babysitting adventures were more than enough to help me realize all the time, effort, and money required to raise children. Sure, the kids were sometimes adorable and fun to be around, but they also required major disciplining. Every girl should babysit during her teenage years. Babysitting may well provide the best possible incentive to postponing sexual activity.

During my babysitting jobs I saw a lot of poor parenting. Once I actually called my mother to have her bring over food supplies for the kids I was caring for, because there was nothing in the refrigerator but old take out and several bottles of beer. It was truly pathetic.

Witnessing this kind of neglect made me pity the girls in high school who purposefully or accidentally became pregnant. I was hugely motivated to practice abstinence—not the easiest thing to do when you are surrounded by friends engaging in sexual activity, insisting that you are missing out. One of my best friends discovered she was pregnant by a boy who had also impregnated another teenage girl. Her life changed instantly. It was about this time that I focused my energy on finding work and didn't look back.

My first job outside of babysitting was waitressing. It was a great job for staying in shape—lots of walking and lifting of heavy dishes. Unfortunately, waitressing didn't retain my interest for long, plus the hours were not convenient. Consequently, while continuing my full-time position at the restaurant, I attended night school at a local Business and Technology Institute. A year later, I landed a job as a Legal Assistant in an uptown law firm. The challenge, money, and hours were much more to my satisfaction; I was also finally on my way to independence, even though I was still living at home.

My heritage is a combination of Spanish, Mayan Indian, and Mexican American. It is traditional for people of my ethnicity to rarely leave the nest until they are ready to build one of their own and fully occupy it with little ones. My father's opinion was especially firm on this subject—more so than my mother's, which I found interesting. Mother insisted on the importance of women having financial security. Based on my own observations, I was inclined to agree. Growing up on bases surrounded by military wives was a lesson in dependency. There was very little opportunity for those who aspired to more than being full-time mothers.

Motherhood is probably the most demanding job there is; I certainly observed how hard my own mother worked to make our household a home. She put her heart and soul into raising her children. In return, she never expected much, other than the love of her family.

I recall waiting for my mother during one of her beauty salon appointments. All the military mothers were chattering away about their marital problems. Money always seemed to be a big topic of discussion. The husbands made the money, and the wives depended on their husbands to dole it out. Something didn't set right with me about this arrangement.

Why were mothers considered second in command?

Observing mothers on the bases and while babysitting dramatically influenced my own desire to have children. I had experienced the hard work and expense involved in caring for and teaching kids. It appeared to be a trap; once caught, there was no release. The curiosity of traveling down that road ceased to exist. If I had taken that plunge, not only would my freedom be curtailed, but I'd be broke! No temptation there.

A Long-Distance Relationship

Nicely settled into my new career as a Legal Assistant, I felt my desire for an intimate relationship grow stronger. There were several girls at the office who frequented the local nightclubs in the area, and it wasn't long before I was included in that circle. The following months were spent prowling the nightclubs and dancing until the early hours. These nightly adventures temporarily soothed my restlessness. Perhaps the yearning I felt was a direct result of the stagnation, a lack of change in a life that had previously transitioned on a regular basis. Nonetheless, finding the right mate was my next challenge.

One Friday evening after work I received a call from a friend inviting me to meet her for Ladies Night at a local hotel lounge. Not feeling overly enthusiastic—the workday had been hectic—I reluctantly agreed to meet her. That night, twenty-five years ago, I met the man with whom I hope to share the rest of my life.

I consider myself to be one of those lucky individuals who found love prior to the explosion of information technology. Finding a mate can be a rather interesting hunt these days—as I'm discovering through my single and divorced girlfriends. Technology has a way of pushing our lives faster and faster, with the emergence of e-mail, Internet dating services, speed dating, and social networking. Today, dating resources are literally at your fingertips.

We sat close to the stage, where a great jazz band was performing. At a table behind me, enjoying the music, a man sat by himself. He didn't appear to be on the hunt. Occasionally, I'd turn around to try to catch his eye, and although we noticed each other, neither initiated a move. Using the sneaky approach, I convinced my girlfriend to ask him for a dance so I could get a closer look. She was much more experienced than I at this sort of thing. After the dance she invited him to join us at our table. We hit it off almost immediately.

We ended up spending the next several days together sharing meals, biking, floating the river, and just enjoying each other's company. Eric, who lived in Seattle, Washington, was in town on business for a few days. Because he was an out-of-towner, I had the idea in the back of my mind that things would not work out—long-distance relationships seldom do. So I thought, why not enjoy the romance of it all?

One sunny afternoon we took a drive to a local man-made beach park and had a picnic. During the course of our rendezvous he asked me an interesting question. "Do you want children?" Being in my twenties, I could not pinpoint all the reasons behind my lack of desire to procreate; I just knew I was not interested.

"No, never had the desire." I said, shaking my head slowly.

"The idea of raising children never really appealed to me, either," Eric responded.

We drove back from our picnic in silence; we both knew what we wanted. The men I'd dated previously seemed to be adamant about eventually wanting children, but this man's interests and goals were in tune with mine—a great foundation for a relationship.

Over the next few months we kept in touch via love letters and phone calls. Although I enjoyed our exchange, I felt that if the relationship were to progress any further I would need to be more assertive. Thanksgiving was around the corner so I invited him to meet the family. My parents welcomed him with open arms, and they hit it off almost immediately. Either they approved of him overwhelmingly, or they were anxious for me to leave the nest; I'm still not entirely sure.

In the spring I visited Eric in Seattle to meet his family. His father welcomed me with open arms, but his mother approached me cautiously, as mothers tend to do with the girlfriends of their one and only son. In time she warmed up as well. Before long, I began hearing the faint melody of the Wedding March and started fantasizing about a wedding.

A "Not-So" Traditional Wedding

At the time, marriage was necessary for me because of the commitment factor. Patience not being my strongest suit, I opted to pop the question myself. As we were dining out at one of our favorite restaurants, my new love wondered if I might consider relocating to Seattle. In other words, he was hinting at moving in together! At that time, Eric was surrounded by divorce; his two sisters' marriages had failed, and his parents had separated after thirty years of marriage. Quite certain that the topic of marriage would not be enthusiastically received, I approached it cautiously by inviting him out for an Italian dinner. That evening, in the middle of my Linguine Carbonara, he asked if I had thought any more about his proposal to move in together. After two sips of Chianti, I began to explain to him that marriage was the only way I could possibly consider moving to Seattle. It was nothing personal—just the way I was raised. I realized I would be the one taking all the risks. Relocating to Seattle meant leaving behind an established life in Idaho, complete with family, friends, and a career. My rather convincing argument was greeted by an all-consuming silence. To alleviate the pressure building in his head, I suggested he ponder the idea until our next rendezvous.

The next day he went back to Seattle. It had been a huge gamble for me to mention marriage, and I wasn't sure I would ever see him again. Some guys are really turned off by assertiveness of this nature—this I understood. But I knew what I wanted and wasn't willing to compromise.

The next two months we continued to communicate via phone calls and hand-written letters. And finally, after what seemed like an eternity, he came for a visit. That evening he presented me with a diamond ring, which I have worn ever since.

Two months later we decided to elope. We considered a big traditional family wedding, but there were many obstacles—the distance between our families and friends, his parents impending divorce. It just didn't seem right to have a big wedding. We wanted a happy occasion, one without worry or chaos—a ceremony to remember. Perhaps it was selfish to plan a wedding designed to make us happy, but isn't that how weddings should be?

We were married at The Little Wedding Chapel in Lake Tahoe, and it was wonderful. Wearing rented wedding finery, we proceeded down the aisle accompanied by "Wedding March" organ music. Despite a slight bout of the giggles caused by nervous anxiety, I managed to complete the ceremony with a kiss and a toss of the bouquet at the video camera set up at the corner of the chapel. In lieu of a reception, we went to the dinner showroom of the Hilton Hotel for an evening of entertainment. It wasn't the wedding most women dream about, but for this woman, it was perfect.

Arriving back at my parents' home several days later we packed up the last of my belongings and headed out on our new journey, the journey of a married life. The prospect of relocating in Seattle as a new bride was very exciting. It wasn't until the day of our actual departure that I realized one of the consequences of this new chapter in my life: leaving the family I'd spent my entire life with.

I remember sitting on the couch in the living room with my parents, busily preparing for my departure. It was then that I realized this was "goodbye." My legs turned to cement and wouldn't allow me to lift my body from the couch. Observing everybody's happy faces, I realized I was the only one not smiling. To spare my parents and my new husband the sight of me breaking down like a weeping child, I rose to the occasion and hugged and kissed my father, my mother, and even my brother. We took photos before we departed. It was a bittersweet moment.

We all waved goodbye. I took one last look back through the window of my husband's car and we headed to The Emerald City of Seattle, our little U-Haul trailing behind us. As I sat in the passenger seat hiding behind my big Jackie O sunglasses, tears filled my eyes and the pain in my belly grew stronger. Once again, I was experiencing the pain I had felt so often during "a departure"; this time, however, the sense of loss was profound and would revisit again intermittently over the next twenty years.

I didn't realize how much leaving Idaho would take me on a journey into a world I was unprepared for. I was no longer a "single woman" and my new status as a "married woman" carried with it the burden of new expectations. I have encountered prejudice based on my heritage, my gender, and my military status, but never in a million years would I have guessed that the prejudice that would haunt me most would center on a "choice" I had made and felt quite certain about.

The Stepford Wife

Shortly after our arrival in Seattle we purchased a single family home. Since my husband's business involved regional sales and service, he was required to travel quite often. In view of the fact that we had agreed not to take the procreation path, we saw no reason to combine incomes and share a checking account. I had saved a small nest egg from my previous years working as a Legal Assistant, so shortly after our marriage I decided to take time off from work, while still contributing toward household expenses. Initially, it was fun traveling from city to city with my husband, staying at nice hotels, sleeping in, ordering room service, and reading books beside the hotel pool. I enjoyed playing the "Stepford Wife" role.

During this phase of my life it was important for me to take care of my man. In the back of my mind, I desired independence and a career, but at the start of our marriage I took pleasure in the domestic goddess role, as long as it wasn't "expected" of me. Creating new culinary dishes and decorating our home satisfied my creative side. However, I soon tired of the role, and my yearning for something more grew stronger.

To accommodate my husband's business trips, I pursued short-term assignments with a temporary agency. The autonomy really appealed to me, and with each new position I gained experience, attained new knowledge, and met interesting people. I encountered women whose careers ranged from engineers, managers, marketing directors, to top level executives. Each was confident, driven, completely independent, and displayed an attitude of "anything is possible." After being in the presence of these women, I began comparing myself to them and questioning my own career choices. The bar was suddenly raised.

One of my temporary jobs landed me in a Fortune 500 company supporting an Executive as an Administrative Assistant. The cubical community of the corporate world was challenging and competitive but offered a wealth of opportunities, which eventually led me to establishing a permanent career of my own. After several months, I was offered a full-time position. My immediate concern was, how would I accommodate my husband's business travel schedule? The new job meant we would have to spend more time apart. Knowing this to be a sensitive subject, I made reservations at one of our favorite Greek restaurants.

As we indulged in our Mediterranean Calzones, I recalled the night we'd discussed marriage; that had eventually turned out the way I'd hoped. My concern was short lived. To my surprise, my husband didn't hesitate. He agreed that it would be good for me to pursue my own career, and said that we would find a way make it work. Apparently my desire to grow had been reflected in my mood swings during the past year, and he realized this opportunity could change that.

Eagerly arriving at my "temporary position" the next morning, I approached my boss with a huge smile on my face and happily accepted the job offer.

The Biological Mock

Fitting into the corporate clique was not easy, particularly for someone who has chosen to live a different lifestyle than her peers. Not only did I have to deal with the competitive side of the corporate world, but also the family-oriented issue. The usual topic of the day around the coffee station involved kids' issues or accomplishments. The proud soccer dad describing in vivid detail his daughter's winning score during the last few seconds of the game. A few mothers discussing the best baby food or diaper rash ointments. Then there was the ultimate downer of the day:

"So Patricia, when are you and your husband going to start a family?"

The question was asked as if I had no say in the matter; having children was just considered to be part of a woman's process, like when she starts her period, or when she goes through menopause. It was expected that one day I would wake up and discover I was pregnant.

My usual response to this personal and intrusive question was, "Oh, we'll probably start a family within the next year or two," simply to avoid the topic. But I wasn't comfortable with such dishonesty. It wasn't just a little fib, but an outright lie. The busy bees would eventually swarm over for another sting anyway, so why bother continuing the façade? It was my choice, and if people refused to accept me because of it, so be it.

We have all been forced at one time or another to take an unpopular stand that might affect the rest of our lives, whether it's deciding to cohabitate rather than marry, to forgo college, to move away from our immediate families, to remain childless. My biggest challenge was not only "accepting" but "owning" my choice not to procreate. I also realized my Latin descent would make people even more likely to assume that I would have a large family.

A few weeks later at the coffee station, I poured myself a cup of coffee while another group of employees were chattering away about their kids.

One of the ladies noticed me and asked, "Patricia do you have kids?" Smiling, I simply said, "No." She responded, "Well don't let your biological clock pass you by ..." (Chuckle, chuckle.)

Out of the blue something snapped within me, forcing me to cross over to The Dark Side, or so it seemed. Summoning my courage, I simply smiled and said, "You know, we've been seriously considering not having children."

There was an uncomfortable silence, as if somebody had just broke wind. I continued, "Neither one of us has a burning desire to raise kids. Quite frankly, we both just really enjoy our freedom." Staring back at me, the wide-eyed questioner did not respond. I smiled, turned around, and walked out of the room, feeling both relief and newfound strength.

The feeling was very liberating. To this day, I haven't been able to deliver a good one-liner for the baby question without wondering at the personal reasons behind my own decision. There isn't one good answer that will satisfy everybody's curiosity. I have learned to accept that I will always be asked to explain myself.

I mean really, do we force people to explain why they chose to have children?

A Balanced Life

How do I feel about my choice today? This is not a topic I spend much time pondering. Rather than dwelling on the past, I try to live for today. The journaling process has revealed areas of my life that require more attention—passions discovered in my youth that have been neglected as an adult. To date the majority of my adult life has revolved around education and career, priorities my parents encouraged.

I am my father's daughter; I have chosen his path over my mothers'. I am proud of my father. He enlisted in the service right after high school and managed to work his way up the highest level in the Air Force ranks in an amazingly short time. When he finally retired he established a second career in a Fortune 500 company and achieved a high-level management position. I guess some people are born leaders. Like my father, I have a satisfying career in Research and Technology working for a Fortune 500 corporation. I am also pursuing my PhD, thanks to my mother, who thought it important for me to push myself to the highest education level possible. Perhaps her wish for me was inspired by a few regrets she never shared.

My mother took another route. Following the lead of her generation, she passed on her personal dreams to dedicate herself to her family. Being a mother is enough for many women, and I hope she was one of them. If I had been she, maybe I would have felt compelled to do the same. Those were different times. But I would not have accepted my lot with anything like her grace.

Because I did not have children, I've been freer to explore my creative side and travel. Fulfilling these two passions are as important to me as food, water, shelter, and love. Without it, my spirit feels deprived. Being an Air Force brat planted the wanderlust seed. My zeal for life is directly associated with traveling. To physically explore other countries is the best way for me to learn and understand other cultures. Fortunately, my husband shares this passion and we have been on quite a few adventures during the past twenty-five years.

Although my husband and I can't claim her as a dependent, we do have a darling little being in our care. Her name is Coco, and she is a Morkie (half Yorkie/half Maltese). It took us twenty years to commit to adopting a dog, but we finally did it. This new family member has required a bit of an adjustment, but she has greatly enhanced our lives by giving us unconditional love, devotion, and entertainment. Our love for dogs in general led us to volunteer at the Humane Society. As long as I live, I will always have a special place in my heart for dogs.

If I am fortunate enough to reach the age of retirement, I still plan on keeping up with my career. There will be no grandchildren in the picture, but I am Auntie Patty to my nephews and look forward to eventually becoming Great Auntie Patty some day.

From the time my nephews were born through their teenage years, we have had many fun times together. They seem to have an endless supply of energy and ideas. As I watch them age, I witness the complexities of modern parenting. My brother and his wife enjoy sharing stories about their mischievous sons, but some of them validate my choice not to have my own children. Like the time Zak came downstairs from his bedroom and casually asked his parents, "Has anybody seen my snake?" Or the time Richie placed stretch wrap across the toilet bowl. Need I say more? Spending time with my nephews keeps my life balanced. But after I return them to their parents, I enjoy the peace and quiet.

My husband and I feel very fortunate to have the best of both worlds.

Renee Ann's Journal

A Religious Upbringing

I was raised in a typical Protestant Christian setting. My parents were devoted to an unwavering acceptance of the doctrines of the 66-book Bible, the Protestant teaching of Sola Scriptura—a Christian practice that has its origin in the Protestant Reformation, stating that "Scripture is the only inerrant rule for issues of faith and practice"—and many other Biblical interpretations that date back to Martin Luther, John Calvin, and other Protestant Reformation leaders.

As a child, I was naturally inclined to believe everything my parents believed, as well as the views endorsed by our local church, Pastor, and a selection of contemporary Protestant leaders. I accepted that everything I was taught was totally right, true, and free of error. I was also taught not to question or doubt those beliefs. Furthermore, I was discouraged from asking questions about my religious views and reading sources that might challenge those views. Throughout my twenties, my religious outlook underwent a metamorphosis of sorts as I learned more about the world and incorporated this knowledge into my new frame of reference.

I do not see the world as rigidly as I once did.

An Unpopular Teenager

My father was born and raised in the Northwest and came from a very conservative family background. My mother, born and raised in the Deep South—the Bible Belt—ironically had parents who never went to church and who were both registered—though not excessively liberal—democrats. My family also included my two brothers, Randy and Ronnie. Though I have always loved my entire family tremendously and am blessed to be a part of it, I realized early on that all family members seemed to prefer my younger brother, Ronnie.

The only way I can truly describe my relationship with Ronnie is that we thought alike. Our conversations flowed so rapidly with such perfect understanding that communication always felt effortless. A great many of the opinions I have today stem from my time with Ronnie, from our seemingly endless conversations and the events we experienced together.

Not only was Ronnie my favored family member, but I loved him more than any other. I have spent more time with Ronnie than any other person in my life. I was nearly two years older than he, thus the leader. He would follow behind me, desiring my approval, and he kept all the secrets I ever shared with him.

We were both unpopular at school, with rather desolate social lives. Our social isolation helped fuse our lasting, covalent-like bond. During my grade school years, I only had one female friend who became my absolute best friend. Perhaps I enjoyed her friendship so much that I never felt the need to establish more female friendships. Perhaps having brothers made me naturally more comfortable around boys. I did feel that most of the girls in my school were too heavily steeped in their cliquish, elitist ways. They also seemed entirely too catty and shallow; they were always so concerned about clothes with brand names, perfectly matched and expensive. Heaven forbid if someone's outfit didn't match! She was immediately chastised.

This early exposure to the "mean girls" of the world drove me further and further away from pursuing female friendships.

My reclusive ways were also the result of my dissatisfaction with my appearance my natural discomfort in the social sphere. I found the implicit demands and expectations of the popular crowd burdensome. Bowing to their repressive conformity was an integral part of being popular. I certainly didn't have the physical or mental attributes that would allow me to conform to the "popular" standard.

As the years passed, I noticed more and more how severely I lacked the interpersonal skills necessary for interacting effectively with my peers. I was impulsive and awkward. Additionally, during my early teen years cystic acne began to cover my face. In the ninth grade, my fellow students told me unabashedly how ugly I was. Their words and actions were so pernicious and deeply scathing during that period that I still feel uncomfortable discussing them today. Their persecution led to entrenched feelings of grief, bitterness and self-loathing.

Though I still feel a strong aversion to the idea of the "popular cliques" that dominate schools, my life journey through middle school and high school taught me genuine empathy for the outcasts, for those whom society deems inferior. I went through so many years of feeling inferior that I truly understand the immense pain that comes with it. At the same time, distaste for the pressure to conform to the prevailing expectations of society grew within me.

Being a teenager without a social group of friends can be almost unbearable. It is at this crucial phase of life that a search for identity begins. Friendships with one's classmates give teenagers a sense of freedom and reinforces their own newly evolving identity. During this time, my brother Ronnie was my partner and my support in the quest for an identity. Our shared unpopularity contributed immensely to the depth and energy we integrated in our relationship.

Almost every childhood memory and nearly all my memories as a teenager are seared with the presence of Ronnie. He is part of me.

Almost every summer afternoon we would go for lengthy walks out into the countryside. The summer sun and the light breezes wafting through the air would gild the wide expanse of wheat fields with flaming golden ripples. During these times, we felt free from the harsh, impossible demands exerted upon us by the world of our peers. We would converse for hours and laugh at our own absurdities and the absurdities of others. Together we shared a mutual passion for adventure and nature.

The mountains were our preference among the Earth's variety of natural landscapes. During our teenage years we became avid backpackers alongside my father and his hiking buddies. We spent many a summer weekend hiking mountain trails to secluded lakes in the Eagle Cap Wilderness of Eastern Oregon. We adored the chance to sleep outside on summer nights looking up toward the changing stellar tapestry overhead.

We were raised as Christians, though together, away from all others, we would engage our minds in eccentric thoughts and questions regarding the belief system we had been immersed in since birth. Sometimes we would approach our faith with simple, harmless curiosity and other times, with flagrant challenges and impassioned arguments, both of us being on the same side. There was surely no one else to trade ideas with the way I did with Ronnie. From our perspective, it seemed like most people regarded Christianity from one extreme or the other. Ronnie was balanced enough to allow me to vent my ideas and angry emotions regarding certain Biblical passages and Christian doctrine without sentencing me to hell or dismissing the idea of Christianity altogether. His evenhandedness allowed me to develop a comfort with him that I have never known with anyone else.

When you form a unity with someone it is interesting how the world outside of your unity suddenly becomes extreme and eccentric in all its views and responses to certain situations. Ronnie validated my existence, made me comfortable with the "Me" I was. It is a priceless blessing to wander through even a brief interval of life with such a person.

Despite the erosion of self-esteem I encountered during my years in public school, I was fostered by my friendship with Ronnie. At least I had one friend, one who knew me well and yet totally accepted me and valued my presence in his life. I cannot forget our numerous walks, our endless joyrides in the old white truck, exploring abandoned homes together, going for long walks after midnight in the deep blackness of night, hitchhiking all over town on sweltering summer afternoons, and feeling our spirits lift as we listened to our favorite musicians—Metallica, Tom Petty, Enya, and Simon and Garfunkel.

During these years I became quite rebellious. Unlike many other confused, rebellious teens whose bad behavior was compounded by negative discipline, my parents came up with a positive solution, that I be allowed to live in and explore a foreign country for an entire year. My parents predicted that my behavior would only become worse if I were forced to continue living in the same environment.

Acceptance in Africa

I received the news from my parents with great jubilation. It is not difficult for me to recall the memories of this year. They were formed when I was still growing and so were successfully joined into the fabric of my self. Thus, I sometimes feel as if I am part African.

At the age of fifteen I embarked upon an adventure that forever changed me. I traveled far away from my country-life setting to Dakar, Senegal. Dakar is a large city on the western-most tip of Africa. I attended an International/Missionary school, and I was granted the opportunity to live off campus with an American couple in their cement house beside the beach. I was immersed in color and life, the reality of poverty, friendships, and unconditional happiness. I had never known happiness and delight like this before.

Unlike in America, in Senegal I formed many friendships. The people there seemed to accept me without restrictions. I could wander through a neighborhood and instantly make friends. As I passed they would invite me in for sardine and onion sandwiches on baguettes, or for red rice and fish. I was often ushered onto a neighbor's porch and given a freshly brewed pot of Attaya, an incredibly sweet black tea infused with mint leaves. We would entertain ourselves in lively, humorous conversations as we watched the tea maker demonstrate his skill at making tea in traditional Senegalese style. This process involved the back and forth motion of pouring the steeped tea from one cup to another, from a height of at least one foot. The result was a tea with a luscious layer of foam on top.

The best part of Senegal was the people. I developed a love, an intense infatuation for the Senegalese nationals. They were always so open, friendly, uninhibited and devoid of arrogance or any form of pretense.

During my stay in Senegal, I became passionate about learning the local dialect, Wolof, as well as French, the national business language.

When I returned home I missed hearing Wolof and the voices of my newfound friends. I had changed, had developed an African consciousness. It was not surprising to me that I later chose to marry an African.

Culture Shock

Several years later, at the age of nineteen, I met my husband at a small college I was attending in Phoenix, Arizona. I was naturally attracted to his shiny, black skin and the fact that he came from West Africa—a land both familiar and fascinating. Also, I was delighted that a Christian man was finally interested in me. To this day, he is still the only Christian man I have met who was ever interested in pursuing a long-term relationship. We dated for a very short time before becoming engaged and marrying just a few months later.

Though we each had our share of character flaws, the fact that he was a Christian and claimed to truly love me overrode any feelings of doubt in my mind about our relationship. My first mistake was jumping too soon into marriage, but my second was assuming that I had realistic expectations of what a husband would be like.

I come from a family where the men are far above society's standards of what a good husband and father should be. I naturally assumed that my husband would likewise be of this caliber. After we married, the reality surfaced. I realized that the only way to keep life manageable was to continually change myself, usually without success, in order to keep my husband even the least bit happy.

One of the decisions we agreed upon was to have children. Although we used birth control during much of our marriage, we assumed that someday we would have little ones to love, nurture, and guide. When this didn't happen, even after we stopped using birth control, we still continued on with our busy schedules, hoping for children one day.

A couple years later, still unable to conceive, I made my second trip to Africa, along with my husband. We both agreed that it would be good for me to see his homeland of Liberia and meet his relatives. We spent about two months there.

Driving from the main airport to Monrovia, the capital, was a surreal experience indeed. I had never seen this aspect of Africa before—the densely vegetated landscape, so very exotic and verdant in its display. There were no signs of modern civilization anywhere.

As we drove along the pothole-riddled road, we passed many people walking without shoes. Some were carrying unwieldy bundles of firewood atop their heads, others were holding lengthy sticks skewered with dangling fish. It was dusk, and campfires blazed outside palm-thatched huts. Children were everywhere. I saw smiles so very wide and soulful.

We stayed in Monrovia for the first week or so. The entire country of Liberia had been without electrical current and running water for several years. This alone was a major culture shock for me. The infrastructure of the city had been destroyed during the civil war several years earlier. Every single cement building was still blackened from fire and pelted with numerous bullet holes. Loose, crumbling chunks of cement dappled the sides of buildings, surrounding them. Not a single structure existed that wasn't savagely paint-chipped or entirely stripped of paint. The scene served as a vivid reminder of the country's lack of progress ... There had been very little reconstruction since the civil war.

We rented a Land Rover and traveled to the raw interior of Liberia ... through the lush, enchanted rainforests. We would stop occasionally to "use the restroom," which usually entailed an expedition by foot into the rainforest itself. I savored every moment of adventure.

We passed pristine, tropical lakes that were encompassed by coconut palms, banana plants, and other kinds of flourishing vegetation. We traveled alongside jungle ponds that were covered with bright green lily pads with bold, pink flowers sitting on top.

We arrived at the relatives' farm late at night. There was absolutely no unnatural light anywhere. I stumbled out of the Land Rover, suffering from dysentery and trying to maneuver my way out into the pitch blackness to some removed corner where I could vomit freely. After I was able to give in to this urge, I looked a ways farther, and to my surprise, I saw my husband's relatives gathered around a flickering fire. Everyone stared at me wide-eyed, unable to empathize with my condition.

After regaining my composure, I introduced myself to each relative.

The darkness beyond the roaring campfire was occasionally penetrated by flashes from lighting bugs; wildly brilliant stars also glistened overhead. It was getting very late and my stomach was torturing me with sharp, intermittent pangs, so we decided to find a motel for the night.

The next few days were spent relaxing beneath large sheltering trees atop handmade grass-woven mats on the farm. Many of the relatives spoke very little English, so communication was a challenge. I watched as the village women pounded palm nuts into a red oil, a key ingredient in many soups and stews. My husband's relatives owned a large chunk of rainforest near their farm, so we had the opportunity to explore a section of it. The jungle was so thickly vegetated that I could see only little slits of blue sky above. We followed a narrow trail that led through the interior, past spider webs, vines, and little swamps that were supposedly inhabited by a rich abundance of life; including pythons and crocodiles.

Later in the afternoon, the women on the farm made a delicious seasoned Guinea fowl and hot pepper broth to put atop freshly cooked, homegrown rice. My appetite had returned and I received this meal with the utmost pleasure and appreciation.

At the end I was honored with a cup of palm wine, probably the most refreshing, heavenly substance my tongue has ever experienced.

Afterwards I was led around by the children, who were anxious for me to discover their farm. I saw the rice patties, the pumpkin patch, and the pen of Guinea fowl and chickens.

We went into the open cement structure that functioned as the family shelter. The cement walls beside their beds were streaked and smeared with blood. There were no windows or ceilings, so the mosquitoes feasted on their bodies at night. The cement walls themselves were tattooed with blood smears. This made me reflect on the universal solvent, water, and on other resources, like cloths, napkins, and tissues. I normally thought of these resources as cheap or easily accessible, but here they were more of a luxury than a necessity. Fresh, pure water—although present in a couple of giant barrels outside the house—was an extremely limited resource and used very sparingly, even for drinking. Wiping oneself after each scratch would be wasteful.

I could not conclude our trip without visiting the Liberian coast for at least one day. I invited my husband's cousin Aikyah to join me for the beach outing. We had a delightful day together, swimming in the ocean and frolicking about the ginger colored, sandy beach. For the most part, we were alone and the beach was ours. The weather was overcast, and like the ocean water, ideally warm and soothing. High, powerful waves crashed forcefully against the shore and then receded back to sea as if tugged by some fierce, hidden hand.

Several groves of coconut palms nearby made for a shady, peaceful retreat. Upon our request, a boy fearlessly climbed the trunk of a coconut palm and harvested a few coconuts; joyously we drank the luxuriously sweet, thirst-quenching liquid. We had also brought with us a bag of freshly cut sugar cane. One of my best memories of that trip was sitting there silently with Aikyah, enraptured with the light, balmy sea breezes, crushing the succulent fibers of sugar cane with my teeth to extract the candy-sweet liquid.

Liberia offered me a fresh perspective of Africa. The majority of Africa's capital cities host at least a moderate population of foreigners. Monrovia was unique in this aspect: there were so very few foreigners to begin with, and the majority were of Indian or Lebanese descent. It didn't matter where we traveled, whether it was the city, the surrounding villages, or the rural areas; people stared at me with wide-eyed shock. Some of the young children I encountered would run from me in utter fright, crying and screaming. Though I had always harbored negative feelings about my physical attributes, I wasn't quite prepared to see myself as so hideously frightening that I could actually repel little children!

To them I was a scary white monster, a person deprived of color, a sight never before seen. This was an opportunity for insight. I saw myself as both a minority and someone who, in some contexts, appeared very scary. While there are many blond-headed individuals with light colored eyes where I come from in America, these features are indisputably rare all across the African continent.

For the longest time I had thought of myself as boring and common, but after seeing myself through the eyes of Africans I learned to respect and value my own uniqueness.

Of course it is not merely physicality that makes one unique.

Conforming to the desires, ideas, expectations, or beliefs of others when you do not feel ready, interested, or comfortable in doing so is a guaranteed means of decreasing your uniqueness.

Although this has been a difficult process, I am slowly learning to make decisions that reflect who I am and the way I think. I am learning that there is not one decision that will simultaneously please everyone. We as women need to learn that the people we surround ourselves with must respect our individuality; that is just as important as the decisions we make and the uniqueness of our personalities. Just as life isn't perfect, neither are our decisions, but in the long run we will always feel better being ourselves than trying to be someone else. Because we each have different personalities, circumstances, and ways of understanding the world, a "right" decision for one woman will be quite different from the "right" decision of another.

Losing Part of Me

During our first couple of years of marriage, my husband and I lived in Seattle, a five-hour car drive from my hometown of Milton-Freewater in Eastern Oregon. During those years I was rarely able to return home and visit my family. Despite the distance, my brother Ronnie and I somehow maintained a close rapport. In late winter of the third year, I noticed that a couple of months had elapsed since I'd had any contact with Ronnie. One evening I developed an almost uncanny need to contact him. I remember wanting to speak to him so intensely. Never before had I had a compulsion this strong, nor a feeling of such unmatched urgency.

On my way home from work that night I found myself driving to a gas station, where I purchased my very first phone card. That night, just after entering my apartment, I dialed Ronnie's phone number, a new one, since he was now living with a friend. The phone rang many times before he answered. He was actually on his way back to bed after using the bathroom, yet in his fragmented consciousness, he was thrilled to hear my voice.

As he began to arrive back into a fuller state of consciousness, he informed me of his need to get enough rest, since he would be waking early the next morning. In some way, however, our conversation progressed, unfolding into a deeply involved exchange that still stings my memory. We recaptured important moments of our history and reflected upon childhood experiences. We reinforced our own identities, making certain that neither of us had changed, and that our essence was as home-baked as ever.

This conversation felt different from any prior one. Ronnie seemed a serene, peaceful creature with a pervasive meekness and a readiness to admit his shortcomings. He spoke of the characteristics he wanted to improve—like being more accepting and merciful to others—or holding his tongue when he felt inclined to gossip or say unkind things or make snap judgments about people and situations.

His words began to flow in a torrent of meaningful expression that reached beyond feelings and emotions and actually penetrated my spirit. "Life is a vapor." he poignantly stated. "We only have a limited number of moments to live here, so we must decide what we are going to believe and try to live in a way that reflects those beliefs."

I agreed, transfixed by the depth of our conversation. "Do you feel like you are getting closer to God?" I asked him.

"Totally," Ronnie exclaimed in joyful assurance.

Then he told me of his recent spiritual endeavors. He would go for lengthy midnight walks. In solitude he would ponder his existence and reflect upon life and God. He had never been much of a reader, but he had finally picked up his Gideon's New Testament and began reading it for the very first time.

Our conversation ended a few hours later. I expressed my gratitude for being able to speak to him for so long, and told him how very much I missed life in the country and going for long walks with him out in the wheat fields.

A week and a half passed, and I was at home with my husband and his nine year-old-sister who was living with us at the time. Bedtime had arrived when I began to feel an uncanny disturbance in my spirit that translated into a physical pain. It wasn't just my stomach that felt ill or my nervous system that felt off-kilter; it was the intangible faculties—my mind, emotions, and spirit, that felt vexed, yet for no particular reason. All through the night I tossed and turned, waking up every few moments. I paced the house yet could not settle down. I repeatedly asked, "What is wrong with me? What is wrong with me, God? Can't you pacify me at least for tonight?"

Until then I had never taken a sick day from work. It was three o'clock in the morning, and I decided to page my supervisor and notify her that I could not possibly come to work that day. After the phone call, a craving for deep rest came upon me and I returned to bed. I was exhausted from the anxiety-laden night. Sleep engulfed me for a couple of hours. I could feel the time passing as I slept, and I incorporated the endless ringing of the phone into my dreams, my subconscious mind desperately trying to defend against any kind of interruption. I would have continued to sleep had it not been for the loud, intrusive knocks upon my bedroom door.

It was our Liberian housemate. "Renee, your brother Randy needs to speak to you. It's very, very important that you speak to him now."

My body began to tremble. In an effort to control my quaking body, I clasped the phone tightly and spoke with force. "Hi Randy, what's wrong?"

"Have you heard from Mom or Dad yet?" he asked, trying to remain calm.

"No, what's wrong?"

Then came surely the most painful, egregious words that had ever escaped his mouth. "Ronnie was in a car accident last night and was killed."

Initially my mind interpreted these words as meaningless, almost like a temporary event that would have no impact on my future, as if what had happened was only true in the construct of that single spoken sentence and did not have any outside reality. I had to ask my brother to repeat himself about three more times.

Moments later I lapsed into a world of panic and confusion. I screamed loudly, and in those initial moments of realization, the emotion I felt more than any other was anger. When the anger finally dissipated, I sank into the most profound grief. I cried and wailed throughout the day and didn't feel psychologically balanced until many months later.

A few years have passed since this life-changing event. My brother's death has conjured in me thoughts of both the universality and unpredictability of death.

According to the laws of physics that govern our Earth and Universe, all systems are subject to atrophy and decay. Unlike mechanical systems, vital living systems have a definite point at which we can say that they are no longer alive. Although most of us have the underlying understanding that we will someday die, we rarely live this out pragmatically. Perhaps this is because we get so tangled up and constricted within the physical, material realm. We will never have direct, scientific proof that God or an afterlife exists, so we more naturally focus on those matters that we can latch onto, such as our life at the present moment.

However, the brevity of the human lifespan and the complexity of the human mind suggest a value and worth that supersede our present, physical reality. While before I completely believed in the concept of an afterlife, these past few years have brought about a slow, albeit monumental change in my thinking. Now I have arrived at the conclusion that it is highly possible that there is no afterlife. Just as other life forms die, their components degrading back into the earth, I see no reason to believe that humans are so much more special and superior.

Overpopulation

Eventually my husband and I ventured back to Africa, where we would live for six months. This time we chose Ghana, a West African country more politically stable than Liberia. During those six months, my husband and I founded a Christian ministry. I considered it a privilege simply to learn about another African country.

My life in Ghana was a series of highs and lows. As always, I greatly appreciated another opportunity to discover Africa, and even better, to learn about another country. We spent most of our days in Accra, the capital, in a lovely home not far from the Kotoka Airport. The simple, daily routine of driving through the city and observing the many scenes just outside the car window was pleasurable and educational. It was even more exciting to be able to get out of the car and explore the city on foot. We frequently visited the bustling marketplaces, the artisan villages replete with traditional Ghanaian handicrafts, restaurants of all types, and the homes of several Ghanaian friends.

Downtown we detected the continuous aroma of Ghanaian food: fried tomato paste and onions, fried fish, and Fufu, which is a kind of dough made from yam, cassava, or plantain starch that is pounded and boiled. There was also Groundnut Soup, one of Ghana's revered dishes, which consists of cooked chicken or beef and a spicy seasoned broth with a peanut butter base. One of my favorite Ghanaian snacks, which I believe one must acquire a taste for, is Kenkey, a fermented, sour cornmeal that is dipped into a seasoned hot pepper and onion sauce and eaten with dried or fried fish and wedges of fresh avocado. Even now, in my present life, I continue to have occasional cravings for Kenkey.

Despite these highs I was often shocked by the rife poverty and overpopulation. Although I had witnessed tremendous poverty in other African countries I had visited, I saw Ghana as so much worse. The population density probably made this more readily apparent. It was painful to see the multitudes of young street children who had come to the city in search of employment. Many of these children had been taken from their homes in distant villages and brought to the capital, where they were exploited by their employers. This "employer" was usually a family relative or acquaintance who had convinced the parents that their child would be better off in the city. It was normal to see emaciated, malnourished children, some even younger than five years old, carrying heavy baskets of foods and other goods on their heads under the scorching African sun.

The marketplaces were so heavily congested with people that it was difficult and risky to maneuver through them without getting stepped on or bumped into. The market area smelled profusely of sweaty bodies, raw fish, raw bloody meat, and vehicle exhaust.

The seemingly endless masses of people in such untold poverty never ceased to affect my mind and emotions. There was always a brooding sadness that accompanied my visits to the market and a humble admission that life on this Earth could never be fair. I passed by fathers sitting on squalid, city streets, holding their infant children in their arms. I was told, "People are born on these streets, live their lives on them, and they usually die on them as well; it is a cycle without end."

I understood that ultimately I could do nothing to even slightly reverse the cycle of poverty I was witnessing. As I wondered if anyone could do anything, I grew to detest what seemed to be a pervasive irresponsibility that dominated the culture.

Children were being born so rapidly that none of them could ever receive the adequate guidance and individual attention they would need, especially during the crucial early years of childhood.

In contrast to what I saw as irresponsible behavior were the Ghanaian women who worked all day long cooking meals, harvesting vegetables from their gardens, and selling the fruits of their labor at the market. Usually they worked throughout the day with their babies wrapped around their backs. African women have always astounded me with their physical strength and fortitude. I have never seen a particular group of women work so long and so hard, and with such patience. Even more amazing was their decision to accept the hardship of their situation with a positive attitude. Complaining, as I found from my own experience, was considered to be very impolite and offensive.

Another aspect of Africa that I discovered is the corruption of the criminal system. If you have money or lofty connections, the oft-heard cliché *actually* applies—*you can get away with murder*. My husband's sister—an amazing woman and mother of three beautiful children as well as a personal friend to me—was killed by her own husband. He ended up poisoning her with special herbs supplied to him by a witch doctor. The herb, which he secretly mixed in her food one night and coaxed her to eat, did not kill her immediately, but caused a toxic build-up in her liver and execrable abdominal pain. Despite her torment and pains she was able to tell us what had happened. She died several days later, with an extremely swollen abdomen. The autopsy verified that she died of liver failure. However, there was no way to incriminate her husband. We were all aware that he had led a double life as a successful businessmen and husband to a woman in Switzerland, only coming to Ghana for yearly visits to see his African wife and children.

The more I saw the intrinsic hardships and struggles of the developing world—magnified by individuals' irresponsibility, extreme poverty, and a corrupt legal system—the more I wanted to become a responsible person: to clean up after myself, to not be frivolous with money, to develop a good work ethic, to pursue an educational path that is both attainable and intellectually enriching, and to keep my commitments to those with whom I had developed relationships.

Malaria

Probably the most dramatic and frightening experience I had while living in Ghana was when I became infected with the parasitic disease, malaria. Normally my husband and I would remind each other to take our malaria pills every Sunday. During the month of November and part of the month of December, my husband was away in Liberia and I forgot to take my pills for three consecutive Sundays. By the time I remembered, I had already entered the prodromal stage of malaria. Fortunately my husband returned from Liberia just in time to take me to the hospital. Weak and approaching the edge of dehydration, I was admitted to the hospital that night. My fever had reached 106 degrees, yet there was still enough consciousness left in me to take in the hospital environment and to realize that I absolutely did not want to stay there. It was filthy and garbage was scattered throughout the hallways. The thought of needles piercing my flesh in such a disgusting place terrorized me. Though urged by several nurses and doctors to remain in the hospital with an IV hookup, I refused their advice and insisted on being taken home.

That night and the following day were some of the most physically torturous hours of my existence. My muscles ached terribly and my skin was flaming hot. One of the worst symptoms of malaria is the implacable nausea. During this time I tried to drink plenty of liquids, but I could not keep anything down. My recurring fever and constant sweating had certainly sucked out great quantities of liquid from my body's cells. My parched tongue and mouth had been desensitized long ago; now every cell in my body was desperately crying out for water.

When my husband returned that evening, I had finally come to the realization that my body was in an extremely critical state; I would surely die, maybe even within a day, if my dehydration was not treated. Not far from our house there was a little clinic, which my husband had discovered on our route to the hospital. We stopped by, in hopes that there would be an opening. Miraculously, space was available and I was quickly admitted, taken to my own room, and given an IV. To this day, I cannot forget how relieved I was to feel that IV inserted into my arm. I spent the next week in the clinic recovering and being administered anti-malaria drugs.

Looking back, I am grateful to have experienced malaria. The occasional reminder that we, as human beings, are frail and always in death's proximity is good for us, and sometimes even necessary for our growth. Experiences such as my illness and Ronnie's death have helped me gain perspective in my life.

The life I lived in Africa was a portal to a new and intriguing reality. There my previously sheltered senses and limited perspective were opened to a different world having its own unique phenomena, its own definition of morality, its distinctive standards of propriety, and its own mannerisms, ideas, and cultural values. On a grander scale, each country's predominant religion dictates the culture of that country. Discovering how all these variables worked together served to skew the rigid lines of the more familiar western-style Christianity I had known for so long.

Although at this point I didn't abandon the belief system of my childhood and youth, I experienced a wider range of possibilities. Instead of denying the teachings and miracles of a particular religion, or the love and happiness that radiated from those individuals practicing it, I chose to enter into lengthy dialogue with each soul, acquainting myself with these individuals on a closer, more personal level. I thus formed many enriching, connected relationships. I was able to overcome any "I am right, you are wrong, you must agree with my beliefs if you want to be my friend" attitude. Through this experience, I began the slow process of realizing how very little I know.

Humble and Independent

Those raised in Christian households learn a great many ideas, values, and philosophies that differ substantially from those learned and experienced in other environments, religious or nonreligious. Many Christians believe that true spirituality requires us to be dependent on both God and others.

This belief lies at the core of Christianity. I may pursue a certain goal, but Christianity reminds me that my own efforts are not enough. A complicated array of variables exists outside of me and my raw pursuit, enabling me to grow as a person. Christ, as well as other spiritual leaders and philosophers throughout the ages, taught us to appreciate what we have been given, and to recognize the many others, both divine and human, who have contributed to our success and prosperity. This mindset is beneficial because it leaves no room for pride or arrogance.

Growing up, I immensely valued the Christian philosophy of dependence and its ensuing humility, especially when considering the hardship, pain, and added friction that a prideful attitude frequently begets. At the same time, however, I cannot discount the importance of independence in today's society, particularly for women. I believe it is possible to live a lifestyle that is both humble and independent.

Since we do not inhabit a Utopian society, it is impractical to rely on dependence. The need for self-sufficiency would not be as important if everyone were equally trustworthy. Sadly, we live in a world where some of its inhabitants will inevitably cross paths with us, disappoint us, and use us for their own agenda. There are times when we end up giving our trust to people too soon.

If there is one lesson I learned from my first marriage, it is the value of independence. Because I trusted in the viability of my marriage, I didn't bother to invest any of my time, energy, or resources in the process of becoming independent. I did not demand my own bank account in order to save a portion of my paycheck in case of emergency. I did not consider the possibility that I would suddenly be alone and solely responsible for myself. Instead, my husband assumed dictator-like control over our budget, credit cards, and general finances. When I did try to hide small increments of cash for future access, I was eventually discovered and the uproar was worse than living in a state of constant financial uncertainty.

Our financial limitations prevented us both from attending college at the same time, so we decided that my husband would go first; I would begin college classes after he graduated. I hate to admit it, but for the first couple years of our marriage, I was even forced to do large amounts of my husband's college homework. He was working two jobs and I was working only one job, so many of his assignments were doled out to me.

After several years of both of us exerting effort, energy, and finances toward his degree, he finally graduated. Though we had experienced considerable marital discord from the outset, it wasn't long after his graduation that our marriage began to deteriorate irrevocably.

Intertwined with the relational and financial struggle was our inability to conceive. For most of the four and one-half years we were married, I did nothing to prevent pregnancy, yet I did not become pregnant. I still hoped to have children, and after a while I became frustrated and ashamed. I often felt that this inability to conceive was my fault.

What made the situation worse was the fact that I had married into a culture where family and children are of paramount importance. The relatives on my husband's side constantly lambasted me with questions such as, "When are the two of you planning to have children?" I had no answer. I had always been ready and willing to have children, but it was simply not happening. I also feared that I might, in fact, be infertile.

Fortunately, because this marriage was childless, I was better prepared and equipped to leave a harmful, failed relationship without feeling pressured or obligated to make the marriage work "for the sake of the children." Thus my inability to conceive, particularly at this time, actually provided me an easier, more attainable path toward independence. I am now exceedingly grateful for this outcome.

The Path Ahead

After my husband and I separated, I returned to Eastern Oregon to live with my parents. For several months, I felt as if I was at one of the most dependent phases of my life. It was strange to go from several years of being married, working, and having my own car to the sudden change of living with my parents and not enjoying any of the typical privileges of adulthood.

It seemed as if my life was going in reverse. Now that I had tasted freedom, my current situation seemed worse than before; for several months I was dependent, yet I retained the knowledge and experience of semi-independence. Ironically, this new state of dependence allowed me, empowered by family and friends, not only to approach the threshold of independence I had known before, but to travel beyond it. I was finally able to distinguish between semi-independence and true independence.

I had been trapped and constrained in a relationship that had no potential for improvement. I had deceived myself for several years, endlessly blaming myself for all our marriage struggles and persisting in the belief that our relationship dynamics would get better someday. I didn't realize that some people never change or that some situations are impossible. Our only option is to remove ourselves.

A New Direction

The anguish and torment of my teenage battle with cystic acne catapulted me into a future in skincare. More than the acne lesions themselves, the residual patches of crater-like scarring on my face led me to seek various skincare treatments. I found a little skincare spa where I absolutely adored my esthetician. She was also the owner of the spa and had many skincare tips and tricks.

An esthetician is a state licensed skincare professional who treats various conditions of the epidermis. Treatments performed by an esthetician might include chemical peels, microdermabrasion, facials, hydration treatments, relaxing facials with a décolleté, face and neck massage, body scrubs and waxing services.

I didn't have a job at the time and had very little money, but my esthetician was willing to take into account my financial situation. Together, my esthetician and I decided on a microderm series where I would come for a microdermabrasion and peel once a week for a couple of months. I definitely noticed a reduction in the depth of my acne scars.

Thanks to my esthetician's warmth and expertise, I decided that I wanted to move in that direction myself. I ended up moving to Seattle, Washington, and attending a Skincare Institute. There I earned my Washington State esthetics license.

Not having children has given me a unique opportunity to pursue a variety of interests. In addition to working two spa jobs, I have also nearly completed pre-Nursing classes. My dream job is to work for a plastic surgeon and learn about more invasive skin modification techniques.

During my free time I enjoy reading nonfiction books about science, sewing, gardening, and cooking and listening to formal debates online. These pursuits allow me to reevaluate my philosophical position on various subjects. Lately, I have been dabbling in acrylic painting. I love the way that art gives full expression to the mind of the artist with so few boundaries.

As much as possible, I try to lead an enriched, multi-faceted life.

Beyond all my interests and career pursuits, I have found my most supreme pleasure in learning. One of the main things that separate humans from other animals is the ability to learn, to reason and analyze the world on a more profound level. Because of our unique ability, I feel that humans are obligated to learn as much as they can during their brief time on earth. With this knowledge, we can do so many beneficial things, whether it is finding a cure for an illness, increasing our understanding of science and technology, exploring creative ideas that may instigate creativity in others, or just learning how to be happier and more at peace with ourselves. Knowledge and learning have given me more tools to cope with life's challenges. I hope that I will always have the means to take classes on the side, regardless of my current career.

My newfound independence is far superior to the "independence" I thought I had in my marriage. I now have the ability not only to work and earn an income, but to determine, totally on my own, how I will spend these paychecks. My new schedule allows me to take college classes as well as pursue my own interests on the side. My life has never been more fulfilling, never been more enjoyable or liberating. I am thankful for my past because it has made me appreciate my present.

I live today, every day, recognizing that I am in a moment-by-moment, day-by-day process of psychological, spiritual, and physical evolution. I have arrived at a place where I recognize my physical and mental frailty, but even more so, a place where I am learning to accept myself for who I am.

Janice Lynne's Journal

An Old Soul

As the oldest of three, I started babysitting my brother and sister at an early age. I stopped playing with them since I was now considered an authority figure. My parents' friends referred to me as the "little old lady" when I was only five years old. In today's world, the term would be "old soul."

It was also at this age that I declared, "I am never going to date, marry, or have children." Even I had to admit, as I got older, that this was a very strange thing for such a young child to say. I figured what I was really saying was that I wanted to be an independent woman when I grew up.

I was raised in a middle class family. We had enough money to get by, but we always had to watch our spending. I thought it would be nice to be comfortable enough not to have to worry about money, and I would have a better chance at reaching this goal if the only person I had to depend on was me.

As I became older, I thought I could eventually adopt a child, but only when I was financially secure. My first priority was to find a career that would provide independence and financial security. I thought my ambition was the reason for not wanting children, but as I came to realize later, the answer wasn't that simple.

My most vivid recollections from childhood are the frequent trips to see my grandparents. Both my parents are from Salem, Oregon, and we lived an hour and a half south in Springfield. Almost every other weekend, we visited both sets of grandparents and had entirely different experiences. My mother's parents lived in the city, and my father's parents lived on a farm outside the city. Both places offered lots of opportunities to play with cousins and eat a lot of great food. The only thing I didn't like was the long drive up and back. It seemed like hours to me and I was bored to death.

However, the visits were enjoyable because both sets of grandparents spoiled us in their own way. For me, visiting the farm was especially fun. We played in the barn, jumped into hay, and rode around in wheelbarrows, played school to name a few.

In the first grade I set my sights rather high and decided I wanted to be the first woman President of the United States. I even got myself elected the first "girl" President of the First Grade. I read about the presidents and their wives and became quite an expert. I could recite all the presidents from Washington to Nixon. Then I noticed how much President Nixon had aged while in office. Being vain about my looks, I decided not to run after all! I didn't want such havoc and chaos in my life. I could enjoy life and still be productive and successful. I was a natural hambone, so I put my energy into other endeavors.

These were the days of *The Patty Duke Show* in which the actress Patty Duke played twin sisters. I amused myself by convincing my neighborhood playmates that I was twins, one nice and one evil. My scheme was discovered when one day one of the neighborhood mothers asked my mother, "How are the twins doing?" My mother replied, "What twins?"

I was initially devastated when my mother blew my cover. But I decided to turn this setback into an advantage by inventing a new ruse: I would play cousins instead. This gave me an endless cast of characters to portray, limited only by my imagination. I had all kinds of costumes and wigs and disguises, and the neighborhood kids came over often to meet the newest visiting cousin. To this day I do not know if they really believed in all these cousins or if they simply came over to be entertained. As an adult I asked my brother and sister, and they don't know either. I guess it really didn't matter.

We moved a couple times during those years. Each move was at a crucial time for me. In the sixth grade, my dream was to get elected to the cheerleading squad. We tried out in front of the whole school and the winners for the next year were chosen in late May. I was uncoordinated and had to work especially long and hard to overcome my clumsiness. By the time of the tryouts, I had mastered a great routine, complete with a full split at the end. I got elected and was thrilled—until I found out that we were moving to a small beach town on the Oregon coast and that I would be attending seventh grade at another school. I was devastated.

In the new school, which was a lot smaller, they elected the cheerleaders early in the year so I had the opportunity to try out again. I soon discovered that no one had any cheerleading experience or talent, making it largely a popularity contest. As the new girl, I couldn't count on that. The only chance I had was to WOW them with a knockout routine. So I worked even harder, and did I WOW them!

I was on the cheerleading squad from then on—until we moved to Washington State during my senior year in high school—another bad time to move. However, I made the most of it. I had acted in plays off and on throughout junior high and high school, but my senior year was an entirely different story. I had so many credits when I transferred schools that I only had to attend half days. I had the starring role in every play that year and so spent all my time learning lines. I even got Best Actress awards and a small drama scholarship for college.

Acting was my first love, but I never considered it as a career. The prospect of being a starving actor didn't jive with my early goal, to be a financially secure independent single woman.

I simply wasn't confident enough to believe that I had what it takes to make it, either in looks or talent. Even if you are extremely beautiful and talented, the odds are still against you. Furthermore, I didn't want to lose my anonymity and privacy. Becoming famous didn't appeal to me in any way. Paparazzi were not as prevalent then, but society was still celebrity-oriented, and I didn't want any part of that.

In retrospect, I miss the art of acting. The ultimate dream for me would have been to act the part of the first woman President of the United States like Geena Davis did in the series Commander in Chief. That way, I could have achieved all my childhood dreams: I could have become the first woman President without the havoc and chaos, while still doing what I loved and being paid handsomely for it.

Independent Women

This was the sixties, and the women's movement was gaining momentum. I wasn't demonstrating or burning my bra, but the message of independence was in line with my early childhood thinking and affected my beliefs and decisions.

The feminist who had the biggest impact on me was Gloria Steinem. I heard her speak about a woman's right to abortion and the consequences of that right being denied. While I didn't like the idea of abortion, I hated the thought of women determined to abort being forced to go to back-street butchers where many would die. I admired Gloria Steinem when, in the early seventies, she started *Ms. Magazine* and joined other feminists in forming the National Women's Political Caucus. Her many speeches reinforced my determination to be self-sufficient and never to become financially dependent on a man. To that end, I didn't really have time to focus on the women's movement. Instead I focused on finding a way to get there. To me, a college education was the key to a high-paying career.

I had an interest in psychology so I decided to major in psychology and minor in drama. That way I could continue to act. So off to college I went, and believe me when I say, I went the hard way.

My family had no money for college. My dad had been the principal of my high school in Seaside, Oregon. After we moved to Washington State just before my senior year, my parents purchased a business and went into debt.

My first two years were at a junior community college near where I lived, so it wasn't too difficult to earn my tuition and gas money by working part-time during the school year and having a full-time summer job. I babysat infants on campus, was a timer for intramural sports games, and did many other odd jobs. I also worked at a department store and an office supply store. I was a cheerleader for football and basketball during the first year, but had to give that up to work more hours to pay my tuition. I had no time to act in college plays, so I had to give up that pleasure, too.

The real challenge came the third year. I did not reside near a state university and could not live at home anymore, so I'd have to pay room and board. The tuition was also higher. I was determined to get through four years of college in four years, so I had to find a solution. Somehow, I came upon a program called ACTION through Western Washington State University in Bellingham, Washington. You worked at least sixteen hours a week in a job related to social work and attended classes nights and weekends. The employer did not necessarily pay you, but you got credits and sometimes even assistance with tuition. Even better, the teachers came down from Bellingham for the classes, so I could still live at home. The program was perfect for me.

I chose a job with the County Probation Office and became a probation officer for misdemeanor offenses—mostly DWIs. I actually had a regular forty hour a week job and received $200 per month as paid tuition for two years. Because I did pre-sentence investigations and made sentence recommendations to the judge, I had to attend many classes on alcoholism so that I would be able to determine the extent of the alcohol abuse. Can you imagine that? I was only twenty years old when I started, not even old enough to legally drink, yet I was recommending sentences for hundreds of DWI offenders.

Life with Dr. G.

Even though this arrangement got me through the last two years of college and I received my bachelor's degree, being a probation officer was not the job I wanted to do for the rest of my life. The pay was too low, and the work was quite depressing at times. So I had no idea what I was going to do.

During my last year in college I attended an alcoholism symposium at the University of Washington. I had chosen a class given by an Australian psychologist—we'll call him Dr. G. Afterwards he invited me to a cocktail party for the faculty, and I attended briefly. He lived in Philadelphia and subsequently we developed a phone relationship.

When I graduated from college, he had changed universities and moved to Norfolk, Virginia. He suggested that I move to Norfolk, too, where there were more jobs than in my hometown. I had been living with my parents all my life and, now that I had graduated, I thought it was time to venture out.

I got two job offers immediately after arriving in Norfolk: Alcoholism Counselor and State Probation and Parole Officer. The State Probation and Parole Officer job paid more, but I wanted the other. Dr. G. convinced me to take the slightly higher-paying one. I did, and regretted it thereafter. I was in the big leagues of probation and parole: felony offenses. I even had to attend a two-week boot-type training camp along with prison guards. And, because of my extensive training in alcoholism, they gave me the alcohol-related cases.

I was dealing with murderers and rapists and every other felon you could think of. The murderers had usually blacked out and didn't even remember the shootings. This was NOT what I wanted to be doing with my life. I tried finding another job, but it wasn't easy. My path had been set by all of my experience to date.

Finally, after fourteen months as a probation and parole officer, I received two job offers, both in sales. One was in television advertising sales for the Christian Broadcasting Network (CBN) and the other was in corporate account sales for a large travel agency. Dr. G. wanted me to take the CBN job, and I wanted to take the travel agency job. Does this situation sound familiar? It was happening again. Had I learned from the first time? Yes, I certainly had. I took the travel agency job, which put me on the right course for the wonderful job I have today.

Just to make things clear, when I went off to Norfolk, Virginia, to find work, I had a platonic relationship with Dr. G. He had something else in mind, but I was determined to resist. To make a long story short, he got his wish. I married the professor a year after my move. Marrying at age twenty-three went against my life plan. I had vowed to marry in my thirties after my career was established. And my ideal husband would not want children.

A Revelation

Prior to getting married, Dr. G. and I had several discussions about children. I told him adamantly that I did *not* want children. He thought I would eventually change my mind.

Dr. G. had a four-year-old son when I met him. He had brought his wife and son from Australia to California. They divorced after two years of marriage and he moved to Philadelphia. They were fighting, so he never got to see his son. Then his wife remarried and wanted to go back to Australia with her new American husband. Dr. G. thought Australia would be a better place for his son to be raised, so he agreed.

After we married, my thoughts on that issue remained firm. Later, when the subject once again arose, my husband was bewildered. He said he simply did not believe me. I could understand why. When we went to parties where infants or toddlers were present, I was the one to spend most of my time holding the baby. I really do love babies. I just didn't want one of my own. "Why?" he persisted.

It wasn't because of my fear of childbirth or what that would do to my body. I had seen too many women who were mothers and looked great. And women weren't dying from childbirth in America in those days, so that wasn't a fear. Aside from my childhood vow that I would never have children, I didn't really understand my reasons and so could not explain them to my husband. He just thought I was young and would change my mind. I never did. My psychologist husband kept pressing me for answers. Then one day I had a revelation.

During one of our discussions about not having children, I was picturing my four- or five-year-old self talking about not dating, marrying, or having children. I thought hard. Why had I said that? Then another image came into my mind: my mother, surrounded by three very young toddlers—ages one, two, and four. The youngest was crying. I remember my mother appearing overwhelmed. Sometimes she even cried. My mother was trapped by three little babies who were making her unhappy. At that point in my young life, I swore this would never happen to me. That was when I blurted out the infamous statement.

I was relieved to finally understand the psychological reason why I chose not to have children.

An Australian "Step" Son

The moment I met my stepson I fell in love with him. Gavin was so sweet and loving and I could see he needed attention and affection. We started going over to Sydney, Australia, at Christmas when Gavin was seven. Since Dr. G. and Gavin's mother were still fighting, he had to go to court every time we went to Australia to get visitation rights. It usually took a week, so he would fly over a week before me and by the time I arrived his son would be available. We would visit him every year and stay at my in-laws' home.

I thought I might live in Sydney one day—after all, my husband planned to return—so I was glad I enjoyed being there. Flying back and forth was an enlightening experience; I had never been outside the United States before, except for short visits to Canada. Sydney is full of hills and valleys that overlook the ocean or the harbor, and the views are spectacular. Some homes overlook both bodies of water. Everywhere you go, you see another beach or the incredible city skyline. It would be difficult not to fall in love with Sydney. The beauty of the city is overwhelming.

Then there are the Australian people with their wonderful accents. When they speak, it is music to my ears. Australians have to be the friendliest and warmest people in the world. I adored everyone I met. They have a zest for life, and they love to have fun. They have the best sense of humor and their laughter is truly infectious. I had no problem with the idea of living in Australia for the rest of my life.

Being in Australia also gave me a broader view of the world. Twenty years ago, the news on Australian television was so different from our national news. I learned so much more about what was going on in the world by watching Australian news than I could ever learn in America. Most of our news is about us; we gloss over what is going on in the world and focus on how it affects America. I came to realize how much we

Americans consider ourselves the center of the world. What a rude awakening that was for me! In my subsequent travels all over the world, I have continued to gain perspective. Wherever I go, in every other country but ours, I learn more about the rest of the world by watching the television news.

Over the next five years Dr. G. and Gavin's mother were not able to work anything out. When Gavin was old enough to voice his opinion in court, he did so. We had a nasty custody battle in the Australian court, but at age twelve, Gavin chose to live with his father.

Why would he come all the way to America to live with us? I think he wanted to spend more time with his father. His mother had another son with her American husband, and then they got divorced. Gavin was given the opportunity to live with us for a year before going back to tell the court his final decision. How did I feel about raising Gavin? Even as a young girl, I did not have a problem with the idea of adoption or raising a child. I simply wasn't going to bear one.

As I grew older, the idea of adoption became more and more appealing. Considering all the starving children in the world and the dangers of overpopulation, I thought it would be selfish of me to bear a child. Why should I bring another child into the world when I could alleviate the suffering of one? Gavin was that child in need. There was nothing more important to me than giving him a real family. Unfortunately, there was one major barrier to my mission: his father and I were having serious marital problems.

I adjusted well to being a mom that first year Gavin spent with us. His father came home late every night—making money was always his main priority—and I felt like I was the primary parent.

After eight years of marriage, Dr. G. and I separated, and we divorced two years later. During that time I had grown up. I had become my own person with my own philosophy of life. Gavin had been living with us for a year when we separated. I could have easily walked away, but abandoning him never occurred to me. Gavin had endured three divorces in his twelve years of life. I had known and loved him since he was seven. I moved across the street so Gavin could walk over to my condo. He was a latch-key kid because of the long hours his father worked. Dr. G. and I maintained an amicable relationship in order to raise Gavin the best way we knew how. We had family dinners and regular discussions about Gavin. To my ex-husband's credit, he treated me as if I were Gavin's biological mother. And quite frankly, I would often forget he wasn't my biological son. Since I never referred to him as my "stepson," many people thought he was my son. If anyone would ask, I would tell them the truth, but most people did not. It just didn't matter.

After Gavin graduated high school, he went back to Australia for three years of college—the equivalent to America's four-year program. In Australia, if you make the grades, your college is paid for. Gavin lived with his biological mother during this time and then returned to Florida to go to law school and is now a lawyer.

Though I hadn't planned on having a child when I married Dr. G., I found raising Gavin to be rewarding. Even though he isn't my biological son, we could not be closer. I raised him for six years. After he returned from Australia, he didn't need that kind of parenting. He continues to be important to me, and I see him frequently. Recently he gave me the best compliment: "You are the most motherly mother ever."

Never Bored Again

After four years in Virginia, my husband changed universities and we moved to Florida, where I found the greatest job in the world as a sales manager for a major cruise line. It wasn't easy convincing them to hire me. This was the early eighties and the company had never employed a young married woman as a sales representative. The position required a lot of travel and they were worried I would become pregnant. I don't recall the exact conversation, but I was aware of their concern. I didn't want to lose this opportunity, so I assured them that I was not going to have children.

Today, it's laughable that this was even an issue. Many women sales reps have had children during the twenty-five years that I have been with the company. Every birth is a celebrated event, and we welcome a new member to our family. I don't know whether or not they believed me, but I got the job.

What a job it was! As a child, I would become easily bored. Never again.

For the past thirty years, I have been in a race with the clock on a daily basis. I couldn't get bored if I tried. There is simply too much to do. Yet most everything is self-initiated. I worked from home and managed my territory as my own little company.

Since I work from home, the job never goes away. It's right there in front of me, so it's normal to work until bedtime. The only problem now is that time goes by too quickly.

I have really taken advantage of the opportunities I received working for a cruise line that owns other cruise lines. I have sailed on yachts and cruise ships all over the world.

In the beginning of my career with the cruise line, my travel consisted primarily of Caribbean cruises, along with my yearly visits to Australia. Eventually I had been all over the world—to the Mediterranean, the British

Isles, the Baltic, Europe, and Asia. I am especially fascinated with the history of the Egyptians. My favorite cruise was on the Nile, which is so beautiful and exotic. My second favorite is the Baltic—Scandinavia and Russia.

I never could have imagined being given so many opportunities to travel. But having the opportunity doesn't mean being able to do it. Many people on the sales force simply cannot take full advantage because they have families with small children to consider.

I didn't travel extensively during the years I was raising Gavin, although I was able to take him on several short cruises. After he took his bar exam, we spent two weeks on a luxury yacht in the British Isles.

At the time, the job title for the cruise line was Business Development Director. I have found the financial security I so desired. There's a side benefit, too; I have the opportunity to do presentations and seminars for travel agents and corporate groups. Although I'm not acting, I can be as creative as I want in finding ways to generate business.

This is the life I aspired to when I was very young. However, after twenty-eight years with the same cruise line, I threw away my financial security and 401K plan by abruptly quitting my job and joining a small, one-ship cruise company as the VP of sales. To me, this was equivalent to jumping off a cliff. My entire cruise community of colleagues and travel agents were in a state of disbelief. Like me, they all assumed I would retire from this job. After all, in a bad economy, who quits a great job after twenty-eight years? Why would I do such a reckless thing? There are a couple of reasons. The management had changed completely, so I was not leaving the company where I had worked for twenty-eight years, but something very different. Also, I started thinking that it would be a huge shame if I spent my entire life at one company without trying anything else. This move would force me to expand my horizons. It was the most difficult thing I ever done, and I will never regret it. I have been a one-person sales force for three years now and it has allowed me to learn and grow in ways I never thought possible.

After spending all my life in search of financial stability and security, I finally did something that went totally against the grain. No matter what happens in my career, I will always be happy that I took this risk.

Child Substitutes

Since I really do like children, I have sought out substitutes. When first married, I had a small dog named Tina from the pound. She was the runt of the litter and I adored her. I had to give her up because of all the traveling. She found a good home on a farm, but giving her up really broke my heart.

After my divorce I was introduced to birds. I started a new relationship and ended up with eleven small birds. When one of my favorites, Courtney, died of a tumor at only four years old, I was so devastated that I wrote books about her for grief therapy. I published two children's books and a coloring book, *Courtney's First Cruise*, *Courtney's Alaska Cruise*, and *Courtney's First Cruise Coloring Book*. The books were sold on about thirty cruise ships; I also donated many to support children's charities. They were labors of love; I didn't really care about making money. Once I retire, I would like to publish more of Courtney's adventures all over the world.

Over a sixteen-year period I had eleven small birds, who all had wonderful lives and died of natural causes. Each death was painful, especially the last two, because those birds lived the longest. We had such a close relationship that some nights they actually slept on my neck—their favorite thing. I was worried I would roll over on them, but that never happened. I just wish I had a photo, because I'll never know what it looked like having two birds stretched out on my neck.

I have major issues about how people treat their "pets." Animals have feelings and get lonely, and I am concerned that many people do not take this into consideration when they acquire them. What really breaks my heart is the number of pets who are neglected and starved to death by selfish owners who forget to care for them, are too lazy, or simply don't care. I would like to help educate children on how to care for animals and have respect and appreciation for them.

Parental Differences

My parents have had very different reactions to my raising a child. My mother moved to Florida to reside in a condo twelve years ago, because we wanted to be together more than once or twice a year, and she was lonely during the two years after her divorce. The move made me realize I would be taking on the responsibility as primary care taker of my mother, but that was fine with me. My mother visited me for several weeks every year before the move, and now that she lives near me she has seen me in the role of mother. Because my dad has only visited me once—I think Gavin was in Australia at the time—he has not really seen me in this role. Gavin came with me to Washington State once for a family reunion on my dad's side of the family, but that really is the only time my dad has been around my son. By then, Gavin was a young adult.

Gavin calls my mother "Grandma" and calls my dad by his first name.

I talk about Gavin as "my son" to everyone I meet, and my dad took issue with that. He said I should refer to him as "my stepson" so that people don't assume he is my biological son. After giving the matter some thought, I realized that my dad has never seen me mothering, so it is easy to see why he can't relate.

Another interesting issue regarding my parents is their feeling about grandchildren. Even though my brother and sister have been in happy marriages for many years, they have no children. My sister has dogs and cats, and my brother has a dog. My mother doesn't seem to care about grandchildren, but my dad would have loved having them. His brother and sisters have lots of grandchildren, and I wouldn't be surprised if he is very disappointed that he doesn't.

Looking for Love

I have been divorced and single for over twenty-five years. During that time, I had a ten-year relationship with a man eight years younger. This probably should have been a brief rebound relationship, but we developed common interests—birds, wine, and travel—that held us together.

We traveled the world in the heyday of the travel industry at a time when you would be upgraded to first class simply for being in the industry. We cruised on luxury cruise ships owned by my company and were compatible travelers. With all this in common, the years slipped by. He is the only man who ever proposed marriage to me, but it was in the early years of our relationship when I could not imagine marrying again. After my divorce it took me fifteen years to acknowledge that someday I might remarry if I found the right person. I have been looking for that person for the past twenty-five years with no luck so far.

Giving Back

So, what have I learned at this stage of my life? Many things. I have learned that how you think at a very early age impacts your later decisions and the rest of your life. I didn't question why I never wanted children until later in life. I only knew that I didn't want them. I did not care why. I was fortunate to have a husband who pushed the issue and made me become more self-aware. The revelation cleared up my confusion but didn't really change anything. It certainly didn't change my mind. By that time I was raising a child anyway—Gavin.

While I was in my early twenties, my life was all about the need to succeed and have a great career that would give me financial security. I was highly motivated and worked hard to achieve that goal; I was also fortunate to find a job that suited my personality, appealed to my creative side, and provided the stability I so desired.

Eventually I learned that even though financial security and self-sufficiency are important, giving back is equally important. In my case, I was given the opportunity to raise a boy who was not biologically mine and help mold him into the kind of man I admire. Not only is he successful in a great career, he is kind and generous. He has a huge love for family and returns to Australia to visit his biological mother's family on a regular basis. He also spends much time with his father's family, doting on his three young step-sisters and his four-year-old half brother.

Perhaps my role in this lifetime with regard to children was to raise a child who needed me and to continue to give back through my children's books. I would love it if children throughout the world could see through the eyes of Courtney, a mischievous little lovebird who gets into trouble but always learns a lesson. I also want to teach children to be kind and gentle to animals and make them understand what a gift their pets are. Their pets have feelings, too, and need to be loved and nurtured.

I learned by experience to trust my own judgment over that of others. Remember the two job offers I had when I was quite young? The first time I chose the job my fiancé wanted, but the second time I choose the job I wanted, against his wishes. That job led me to the one I have now, so it was a very important decision in my life. Life has a way of giving us the same lessons over and over until we learn them. There are some I still haven't learned, but at least this one sank in.

Another lesson I learned is that most of us fail because of fear—actually many different kind of fears. My fear of becoming a professional actor was a lack of self-confidence and a fear that talent would not be enough. You can never succeed if you don't try. I have had a few regrets over the years, but not many. I have enjoyed life so much. The job I have now is a good second choice to acting and a heck of lot more stable and secure.

I have also known that even though I did not choose the right man for a marriage that would last, he was indeed the right choice in the long run. He led me to my son and to my career.

What do I foresee in my future? I expect to retire from the cruise line and devote my time to writing the rest of my Courtney travel adventure books. I have other projects in mind as well, which involve working with animals and children.

The date of my retirement depends on whether I find a life partner. If I do, I will take his wishes into account. If I remain single, I will probably not retire until age sixty-five, because I really enjoy my job. If I meet a man who wants to travel, and it is financially feasible to do so, I will retire sooner. I still have that travel bug. I have become a grandmother now, a role I enjoy immensely.

I guess the big question is, do I regret not having children? Not at all. Perhaps I made the decision for the wrong reasons, but it ended up being the right one for me.

Stories and Essays from around the World

Twenties

Hannah Conroy, 20
Student
Helena, Montana

I'm twenty years old and have chosen not to have children. When I tell people that, most of them simply respond by saying, "You're too young." But women of any age can appreciate my reasons. It is not that I "don't like children" or am "too lazy and selfish." I was raised in an abusive home and I don't believe I could be a better parent than my own were. Instead of having children myself, I have decided to donate my eggs to women who can't have them. Some might argue that this decision could cause mental and emotional strain, but I don't think so. Donating eggs allows me to help other women, and helping others is what I want to do with my life. It's the reason I'm in college in the first place.

Erin Melkovitz, 20
Paralegal
Ennis, Texas

I sometimes think my desire not to have children goes back to childhood. I can't point to any single event or situation. I just never felt maternal. I mean sure, I love my nieces and nephews to death and am very protective of them, but I don't feel "motherly" toward them and never have. When I was a child, I played with Barbie dolls and toy trucks but I never desired or asked for a baby doll. If I did receive a baby doll as a gift I never played with it. I believe some people have that parental instinct and some don't. I think kids are cute and I don't dislike them; I just don't get all goo-goo. I don't have a desire to pass on a "legacy," as some people call it. And I don't feel like I'm missing out on anything.

Blanka Ignácz, 20

Student

Budapest, Hungary

I live in Budapest, Hungary, and am only twenty years old. I am in college here in my hometown and I study Social Studies.

I am an only child. My parents divorced after two and a half years of marriage, when I was one year old. I've never really asked them about the divorce, but I know that after I was born, they argued more and more.

I honestly don't like children. As a kid and a teen I preferred to talk with adults. I didn't like high school; I had a few school friends but my real friends were much older. The situation is the same now. I especially dislike babies. In my opinion, they are ugly little beings who just scream all day long and can't do anything on their own.

As a teenager I realized that all the girls around me loved babies. They already knew the names of their future kids. I was not interested in this topic. I was about sixteen when I finally decide not to procreate and I wanted to be "fixed" (I still want it!). Frankly, I've never wanted children (not even as a little child), but I was afraid to be judged. First I thought I was weird and that everybody would expect me to have kids, but then I realized I had a choice. No one could force me.

I don't want to ruin my body with the disgusting procedure of giving birth and breastfeeding; I want to spend my money, time and energy on other things. I like my hobbies; I want a good career and I like my calm life. Moreover, I don't want to give up (or "just" ruin) my sexual life. I think babies can ruin marriages and relationships.

Because of my education I know a lot about demography and social policy. The more I learn about social policy models, the truth about the finances of an average family with kids and facts relating to demography, the happier I am to be Childfree. For my personal well-being, I should not have kids.

My mom still thinks I'll change my mind and my dad thinks I need to talk to a psychiatrist. So unfortunately they do not support my decision. Mom wants grandkids and Dad thinks that everybody should get married and have children.

I know that I am very young, so the biggest challenges to my

Childfreedom will come in my late twenties and thirties. At the moment I am satisfied with my decision and hope my family won't drive me crazy.

Jilianne Warner, 21
Linguistics Student
Oulu, Finland

Ever since I was very young, I have been extremely uncomfortable when I have to deal directly with babies and children. I don't know how to talk to them, let alone discipline them, and I definitely don't enjoy being around them. I never really had to make a conscious decision not to have any; it was obvious that I shouldn't.

Experiences have only reinforced my decision over the years. One early incident took place when I was in the eighth grade. The assignment was to write about whether I'd make a good parent. I don't remember exactly what I wrote, but I believe this was the first time I thought in depth about what parenthood entails and how wrong it seemed for me. When I got the paper back, I saw that my teacher had written an encouraging note, something like "thank you for being honest." It turned out that I was the only one in my class who had written that they thought they would make a bad parent. This was the first time I realized that my views on parenting put me in a small minority. I am thankful, however, that my teacher made one of my first experiences recognizing myself as childfree a positive one.

Now that I am older, I have more reasons for not wanting kids. I strongly believe that people should be one hundred percent sure they want children, have the resources to care for them, and be willing to drastically change their lifestyles to accommodate their children's needs. I don't meet these requirements. It's obvious that there are major benefits to not having children such as freedom, money saved, and a happier marriage, but these are only bonuses to me, not the deciding factor.

The only reason I need is the fact that I don't like children and have no interest in being a parent.

Nadya Tretyakova, 22
Student, University of Rennes
France

I think there are some convictions that we are born with. We don't even realize them at first because we are not mature enough. At least that was true for me. I am almost twenty-two now and have understood since early childhood that I would never procreate.

I guess a lot of "normal" people think that people who choose to be childfree had an unhappy childhood or some kind of trauma. But I believe they are often wrong. Of course, every case is unique, so I'll just stop speaking in generalizations and move directly to my personal story.

I was a desired and a loved child, surrounded by loving parents and relatives and the admiration of other adults who saw me as an adorable kid. On the material side, I also had everything I needed. And yet I hated being a kid! I hated that sweet and phony—as Holden Caulfield would say—way the adults spoke to kids. I hated being excluded from the fun and interesting world of adults—those high and mighty people who looked at us top-down—and being relegated to the world of the children, where everything had been adapted (toy cars, toy houses, books and movies for children). This exclusion was, to me, an injustice. Although treated like a little princess, I still felt like an Untermensch, because I was totally dependent on the adults and weak and stupid in comparison.

Children like to ask, "Why?" The chain of why-questions finally led me to the decision to be childfree. I was about five or six-years-old at the time, not older. At that time I really wanted to become an ecologist, to protect the environment and the animals. So I was asking myself: Why are people so irresponsible about the world they live in? Why do they waste everything nature gives them without thinking about the future? And these are people who will have children and grandchildren and so on! Why don't they think about them? Why don't they want to leave a healthy environment for them?

The next question that struck me was: Why do they have children? I think it was after I watched some TV show where a woman complained about being infertile. She talked about how unhappy she was and how she strove to be cured and I couldn't understand her. At that age I didn't yet know all the details of making a child but I had an idea where the babies came out and how painful it was. So I was like: "Come on, lady, you don't have to take the risk of getting an awful big belly with someone in it who will hurt you. Enjoy your life!"

Actually I had a sort of an answer to the question above: I thought people gave birth to kids because life on Earth shouldn't disappear. Humanity had made such great progress, and it would be a pity to abandon all the achievements. I thought the people who had children were the most boring, the ones who felt an obligation to procreate and so fulfilled their mission. I never thought people procreated out of love. I didn't consider my parents to be boring—on the contrary, I admired them as interesting personalities—but I have to admit I couldn't understand why my mother had given birth to me. In my mind having a kid stopped the development of a woman as a personality. So I admired my mother, but realized I would have admired her much more if she hadn't given birth to me (an impossible condition but I hope you understand what I want to say). I am not talking about my father here, because it is the woman's life that is changed hugely after childbirth. Men don't experience the pain of childbirth. As for women, I just couldn't understand this voluntary masochism … So for me my father was a person I admired and my mother was a person I admired and felt sorry for, because she chose to spend a lot of her time taking care of me and not building her career, doing sports, reading books and so on.

Finally I was led to believe that procreation was all about love; people wanted to have babies because they loved them. I could agree with that, having at that age quite a simple idea of love. Personally I loved dogs and wanted one. I did not consider that a dog might not be happy living in an apartment and having to walk on a leash. But then another "Why?" occurred to me. Why are some children abandoned by their parents? And why don't people adopt them first before giving life to new people? Why does that woman on the TV show want her own baby and not an adopted one? So I made a decision: I won't give birth, but I will adopt a child.

The reason for my decision was fear of being different. Actually I didn't want to have a child. I never even played with dolls. But I already understood that it was normal for women to get married and have children; if not, she would lead a miserable life and die alone. And although my perspectives on marriage (also not the norm) and children would probably make me unhappy, I accepted the situation.

At least I thought I accepted it. Soon I realized we would all eventually be dead. I also became aware that life was full of pain (fortunately at that time my experience was limited to losing my baby teeth and having shots, but that was still enough). I was confused. I couldn't build a chain of logic (I appreciate logic and don't like answers such as "just because it is so" or "God wills it"). So, why did people give birth to new people they were suppose to love, knowing that these new creatures would definitely suffer (some a little, others much more) and finally die? Giving life always meant giving death.

That is how I made my decision to be childfree at the age of six. I will never change it. In my story I probably showed the darkest side of my thoughts. I am indeed the person who experiences what the Germans call Weltschmerz, but I am also the happy person who wants to live life to the fullest and enjoy it as much as possible, so there's no place for children in my life. For me it is most important to follow my own beliefs and not be afraid to be different. The most horrible mistakes are made when we do something because everybody does it. I am happy with my decision and believe I will meet a like-minded person who will also enjoy being child-free.

Yuri McMutry, 23
Bankruptcy Lawyer Assistant
Atlanta, Georgia

Just because I am a female and can have baby(ies) doesn't mean I should.

There is hardly anything maternal about me. I don't like children, I'm not having children, and I wouldn't know how to hold a baby even if someone showed me. I don't like being around them, and I try to avoid places with children. Just about every other young person I know has them, but I just see babies/children as liabilities. I want to get my tubes tied, but at age twenty-three, it's difficult to find a doctor who will even talk to me about that, much less perform the procedure.

I do not wish to be a "single parent." I have no issues with single parenting per se, but I refuse to end up as one. If a couple breaks up and a child is involved, more than likely, the young lady is the one stuck with the child. Then there is the issue of child support, court orders, and lots of drama. I'm only speaking as an outsider looking in, but from where I stand, this happens more than not to girls around my age—between sixteen and twenty-five. If I were to have children, I would want to be a wife first, then a mother. That way my family would all have the same last name and grow up in a positive environment. I'm not saying that being married makes you a good parent, but it is a hell of a lot better than just ending up as someone's "baby mama." That is the culture I live in.

If I'm starting a new relationship, I let it be known from the beginning that I don't want children. I have yet to come across a young man who could make me change my mind. A lot of older women get offended or have something negative to say when I tell them I don't want to be a mother. A lot of girls get upset or have attitudes toward me when I tell them I don't have kids already and don't want any. I figure that is because they have fallen into the "baby mama" trap and are unhappy with themselves and their decisions.

They love to say that because I am young, I don't know what the future holds for me, that I should not have anything done to my body because I might meet a young man and change my mind ... I may not be too optimistic about my future, but I know what I do and don't want. If a man truly loves me, he will accept that I don't want kids. This is my story. Hopefully, other young people will read it and relate.

Jay Shannon, 24
Construction Worker
Oshawa, Ontario

[Editor's Note: This story is a departure from the rest. It is written by a young man and it goes into some detail about the process of getting a vasectomy. We decided to include it because it shows that some men are just as determined to remain childfree—so determined that they are willing to take the steps necessary to ensure their decision is permanent. This man got past the false impressions he received from the media about the procedure and the doctors who balked at treating one so young. But we imagine that many do not. This account of his experience may help other young men who are confronted with some of the same roadblocks.]

I have heard a good number of stories about vasectomies: some are actual accounts, some are reasoned speculation and some are wild guesswork. None is close enough to mine to warrant comparison.

I knew from at least the age of twelve I didn't want children. By age fifteen or sixteen I was sure of it. A few months before my eighteenth birthday, I began researching vasectomy as a permanent—nay, the only real—option. My reasoning was that if I were to play with a loaded gun long enough, I'd eventually wind up pulling the trigger, the safety would malfunction and blanks wouldn't be coming out the barrel. I needed a permanent solution.

In the media, vasectomies never seem to be mentioned in conjunction with the "childfree"—not that the childfree movement is ever properly discussed. Through the few instances in media I saw or read where vasectomies were mentioned, I had picked up several false notions about the procedure. I thought that in order to qualify, you needed to be at least thirty years of age, to have at least one child, to be legally married, and to be approved by a certified psychologist.

Not true. In the U.S. and Canada, you need only be eighteen. There are no prerequisites on existing children or marital status. No sperm need be frozen as an insurance policy.

My doctor lives in my childhood town of Belleville, which is a little over an hour from my current residence near Oshawa. As a result, I only see him once every one to two years for a routine physical. When I was twenty-two, I chickened out and didn't ask him about vasectomies. When I was twenty-three, I didn't have time for a physical. Finally, when 2011 rolled around, I told myself I had to take this seriously. The appointment I had made for a physical in February of 2011 was cancelled because of a freak snowstorm. In March I finally made it to the doctor and found the courage to explain my desire to seek sterilization to protect my childfreedom.

My doctor told me he would never stand in the way of a patient's chosen course, and went on to describe the procedure. It is covered by OHIP, but reversal is not, and it is very costly. After two years, the procedure is considered irreversible.

After making sure I understood all that, the doctor referred me to a urologist. He said he would try for one in my area, so I wouldn't have to drive back to Belleville for each appointment. The next day I received a call from my doctor's receptionist, saying the referral had been sent into a Dr. So-and-So, and I should be expecting a call within the next day or two. Two days later, my doctor's receptionist called again to say, "They don't do that procedure." This was a polite way of saying that the urologist took one look at my age and sent it back. But not to worry, I was now being referred to another doctor in the same building.

A few days later, the process was repeated. There were two more referrals before a urologist finally agreed to see me. Of course the doctor was running late, and I was about as terrified as I could be about pleading my case to a complete stranger. Once I made it in there, the entire consultation lasted only ten minutes. The doctor asked for my age, then the number of children I had. I figured that would be the end of it. But surprisingly, he went on. I had to answer the question, "Are you really sure ...?" several times.

Once the doctor was satisfied, he made me sign a consent form, then told me to drop my pants and get on the table. He located the vas and explained what he'd be doing. I would be conscious the entire time, under a local anesthetic. I was free to eat beforehand and drive myself home. I could purchase over-the-counter Tylenol or Advil for any persistent pain. The procedure would last no more than thirty minutes.

I booked a week off work for the surgery, because I am a construction laborer and my work is physically demanding. Had I worked in a cubical farm, I could return to work as early as the next day.

That week was actually a week and a half, because the surgery fell on a Wednesday, and served as my vacation for the year. The procedure involved the usual steps for day surgery—showing my health card, changing into the gown, confirming the right procedure, moving to the next waiting room, etc.

Once on the table, I had a sheet draped over me with a hole for my genitals, and the doctor bathed my scrotum in the antiseptic solution. I was terrified of the one thing I was guaranteed to feel: the initial freezing needle. We've all had that dentist who buys his blunt needles at the dollar store and stabs you five of six times with jittery fingers before it's in the gum, and I figured that's what his would be like.

It wasn't. The needle was a proper surgical needle, sharp as a katana and went into me like butter. The urologist was standing on my right, injecting the left side. The needle and the incision were on the front of the scrotum, just below where the urethra disappears into the scrotum and into the body. I did feel it go in, but the pain was minor and fleeting. Then I felt pressure as the numbing agent was pushing in. The doctor gave it about ten to fifteen seconds, then began cutting. I didn't feel that at all. I was not watching this part, because frankly I didn't want to see it, but I could see his hands moving about.

After no time at all, he said, "The left side's done," and proceeded to the right. He injected the right side, which I hardly felt because the freezing from the left had spread over enough. Then he took the scalpel and moved from the existing incision toward the right, expanding it.

It still didn't hurt, but I could feel the skin tearing. I quickly realized that the left side's freezing would only go so far, and he'd soon cut into fresh skin, so I quickly said, "I can still feel that." He stopped cutting for no more than five seconds, then continued. Now, I could feel nothing.

Again, it was over surprisingly quickly. He pulled out a tool to singe the vas shut at both ends, and as soon as I heard the hissing on that heat on my flesh, I knew it was done, and that I had the best type of vasectomy on the market.

He stitched it up with two stitches, which is all you need on such loose skin. I thanked him and shook his hand, and he told me his receptionist would call in the next few days to set up a checkup to confirm I was sterile.

Although I was clear to drive myself home, I had made arrangements for my brother to pick me up. The freezing would last about an hour, I'd been told, and I wasn't sure if I had any painkillers at the house, so my brother stopped and picked up some Motrin.

About an hour after the procedure, I took one pill—not because I was in pain, but because I was abiding by Motrin's time limits and wanted to make sure I took one by nine o'clock so I could sleep properly. So I took one at five even though I didn't feel pain. I took another at nine, despite the lack of pain, and slept comfortably through the night. The following morning, I still felt no pain and decided not to take a pill until I did.

I never did.

There was some swelling of the testicles themselves (particularly on the left), but they didn't really hurt unless I wore tight pants, which I quickly abandoned in favor of sweats. I was going to the gym by the third day, and masturbating by the fourth. I am usually supersensitive to tactile stimuli, but I think my body realized what a massive favor I did it and decided not to bitch about a little incision.

At the checkup, I was issued two sample tubes and told to collect one sample now and another at least thirty days afterwards. Sometimes, even a third sample is needed because the body needs time to clear out the residual sperm.

For me, only two samples were needed. Both said, "No sperm detected."

I asked the all-important question about the possibility of a self-reversal, and he explained it's about a one in five thousand chance. Then he shook my hand again, I thanked him once more, and that was it.

What a load off my mind! I'm thoroughly and utterly happy with my decision, and I couldn't have asked for the procedure to have gone any smoother.

Britney Paradis Meloche, 25

Paralegal

Montreal, Quebec

Nothing really happened in my childhood that made me decide not to have kids. One day—I was about nineteen—I just realized I didn't want them. I worked at a day camp and two daycares to earn extra money for school, and I noticed kids were a lot of work. It didn't seem fun at all. I am also concerned about the medical history in both my family and my husband's family. I have had hypothroidism since age thirteen and I would not want any child of mine to have to deal with it. There are also many other serious health issues in my family; I could get sick myself or pass them on, and I would not want a child to have to deal with either possibility.

We enjoy our freedom, our ability to do what we want. I am twenty-five and still in school. I enjoy school and I love that I can take the time to decide on what I want to study. My husband will also be returning to school. If kids were in the picture, we wouldn't be able to afford to further our education when we want and for as long as we want. We also like quiet in our lives and enjoy having the option to do absolutely nothing in our free time.

Although I am still young, I am positive I will never question my choice to be childfree. I could not imagine having to devote my life to a child.

Pilvi Salonen, 25
Aspiring IT Teacher
Kouvola, Finland

I always thought I'd have children by the time I was thirty-five. My mother had me, the oldest of four, when she was twenty and my brother, the youngest, when she was twenty-five. I'm twenty-five now, and can't imagine having a mini-me toddling around here, let alone four of them! I think it all started when my sister told me she was going to have a baby. I'd always thought that I, being the oldest, would do everything first (typical first-born mentality, eh?), and then my sister—at the time about eighteen years old while I was almost twenty-three—tells me she's having a kid.

Being surprised is putting it mildly. I always thought that among my two sisters she was the levelheaded one, who wouldn't go and get knocked up by the first guy she started dating. I think my dislike of her partner plays some part in this, too. Especially after I found out he expects my sister to squeeze out at least six kids!

My niece was born in January of 2010, and most of my family's world centers around that little girl. I grow tired of hearing every single poop story from my mother. Yes, my mother, her grandmother, shares every story about this poor girl that has anything to do with poop.

But I digress. About six months after my niece was born my sister informed us that she was expecting another baby. Until then I had only been on the proverbial fence about having kids. But after finding out my sister was going to have another kid, I felt I should try and do something. I'm not exactly sure what my intention was—to prove to her that she wouldn't have to have six kids if she didn't want to and put her foot down on the subject or something entirely different. So I Googled the following:

"reasons not to have children." That is how I found out about another way of life, one that I hadn't heard of before: childfreedom.

After reading as much about it as I could (there aren't that many "official" websites about it, but there are plenty of blogs and articles online), I was still sort of on the fence, but leaning towards the CF side. What sent me jumping to the CF side was something my mother said.

One day, after my nephew was born, my fiancé and I were visiting my parents, and wouldn't you know it, so were my sister and the kids. My mother, who was feeding my nephew, suddenly asked, "So, is [my fiancé's] mother expecting grandchildren any time soon?" I couldn't open my mouth and looked at my fiancé, who was just as surprised as I was. After that I made my decision:

I would not have children.

I dislike the fact that most people think having children is something everyone *has* to do. I don't think you have to do everything just because someone else tells you to do it or because others do these things. I'm not saying that I chose to lead a childless life just to be different, a rebel. I have always been a non-conformist; I enjoy breaking social norms. I made the choice because I feel that I can lead a happier life doing the things I love— not by raising some kids then realizing that I forgot to live life and gain experiences. If that makes me selfish in some people's eyes, so be it.

The next step I took was to discuss the subject with my fiancé. In our relationship, we've always taken a bit lighter tone when it comes to talking about important things, so this was surprisingly easy. I think I said something along the lines of "How about we skip human babies and concentrate on raising animal babies?" He laughed and happily agreed. I've always known that he doesn't really care for kids but cares deeply for animals.

I have yet to "come out" to my parents, as I know what the inevitable conversation will be like, but I plan to do it next time the subject arises.

We haven't really told my fiancé's family, either, but I expect that will be less of a hassle. With luck we won't even have to have the conversation with his family. His mother shared some wise words with us some time ago: "Never become parents; you'll be paying for it for the rest of your lives." We intend to live by those wise words for the rest of our lives, being the last members of the family to share the name of my fiancé's family. That has a nice ring to it, I think … "The last members of this family."

Sarah Anderson, 28
Weekend Supervisor
Wahpeton, North Dakota

I have never been interested in having children of my own. I think my family accidentally influenced me in that regard. Each of my parents have two siblings. My mom has two sisters and neither of them had kids. One was in the Navy and traveled all over the world and always sent me cool presents. They both seemed perfectly happy. My dad has a brother and a sister and neither of them had kids, either. His brother married a woman with kids and his sister was diagnosed as a diabetic at sixteen; as a result she chose to adopt. I was diagnosed at age ten and made that same choice as a teen. Being diabetic is hard and I don't think I could live with myself knowing I had knowingly passed it on to someone else.

All through college I was very open about the fact that I was never going to have children of my own, but I was still interested in adoption. Finally, my senior year of college, I realized I didn't really like kids. The president of the college and his wife had a hyperactive five-year-old and out of the 1,600 kids on campus they picked *my* roommate to babysit the little psycho. I discovered that she sometimes brought him to our dorm room, because one day I found a half eaten sucker stuck to the top of my coffee table. I would become very nervous when kids got in my space. My roommate and I were both theater majors and they (the president and his wife) used us (the theater kids) as a free babysitting service because there were always some of us around in the building. That was so rude. They would drop that kid off randomly and disappear, even the day before finals. It wouldn't have been so bad if they hadn't enrolled the kid in karate; he'd show up in his little uniform and spend the whole time running around trying to kick everyone. I don't know if everyone else was just pretending, but they all seemed to *like* it … saying he was soooooo cute. Luckily I was a technical theater major so I didn't have to put on an act. I would go hide in the costume shop; the shop manager would distract him with candy until his mother came back.

Ironically one of my favorite profs in the theater was also childfree, and I decided that her life looked more appealing than one with a kid like this, 24/7. The other main theater prof had five kids but he never brought them to work or expected the students to provide free childcare services.

Part of the reason I don't like kids is the way people change once they have them. Parents think they can just do whatever they want because they have kids. When Mrs. School President found out our costume shop manager was giving her brat kid candy to keep him from getting into everything she put an end to it ... but she still expected us to watch him all the time so *she* could work. Lots of the others loved kids and were happy to play with him instead of working on costume projects. I thought they were all nuts. I would rather hem pants every day for the rest of my life than have a kid.

So far I have been lucky about not getting bugged all the time about my choice. My parents know that all they are getting is "grand kitties" and they have taken it pretty well so far. I think that is because my grandma (on my mom's side) was ahead of her time. She didn't let anyone tell her she couldn't do something because she was a woman. My aunts think that she didn't really want to have kids but did anyway because that was what was expected of wives back then. Of her seven siblings there were two who didn't have children. That was pretty rare back then.

It helps that my best friend has made the same choice; we have been able to take on the doubters together a few times. She has never had to change a diaper, and that makes me jealous! She just graduated from Vet School and is becoming a pathologist. I tell her all the time that I am proud of her, because her parents don't. They just want to know why she isn't married yet. How sad is that?! Once I had a friend ask, "But what about your purpose in life?" Boy, did *he* get an earful! I finally reminded him that even Jesus didn't have kids, and that shut him up. It was such a ridiculous conversation that I wrote a short play about it.

Michelle Oris, 28

IT Administrative and Purchasing Officer
Bacoor, Cavite, Philippines

As far back as I can remember I have never wanted kids of my own. I am a godmother of some of my friends' children. I am interested in how they are doing, but I wouldn't want to raise them myself. Heaven forbid, if something happens to one of these friends, I'd prefer that the children be raised by their own family members.

I cemented my decision to be childfree two years ago, although I believe the decision was actually made when I was very young. I was an only child for eight years and I do remember that I didn't ask to have a brother or sister. I was content to play with friends or on my own. When my brothers and sister were born, I was not enthusiastic about having a screaming baby at home and preferred to hang out with friends. I didn't volunteer to hold the baby or learn how to change diapers so I could help my mom care for the baby. Now that I am an adult, I don't feel it is necessary to have my own children in order to relate to my friends who have kids. Most of my closest, dearest friends are a few years younger; one of them is gay and also has no interest in having children.

Being childfree is perfect for me. I am living life to the fullest, on my own terms, enjoying every second of it. The world is a big place I have yet to explore. I have different interests from my married friends, such as going to the beach and trying out new restaurants. If I have children, I wouldn't be able to enjoy those activities.

I live in a country that is family-oriented and "kid-centric." I used to feel twice as much pressure. I had a friend, a single mom, who was always telling "cute" proud-parent stories about her toddler. One day I was surprised to hear myself blurt out that I would "love" to have ten kids; meanwhile my gut was telling me I was a liar. Saying those words aloud made me feel uneasy and heavy hearted. After that friend and I had a falling-out, I felt relieved not to have to lie in order to relate with her.

I dream of moving to a place where being childfree is more normal, even celebrated.

Audrey Custer-Coleman, 28
Artist and Student
Vancouver, Washington

When I was young, I never played house—I was never interested in being the mommy, and I can't ever remember wanting to have kids. When other girls were writing the names of their crushes and future kids' names on their Trapper Keepers, I was focused on getting good grades so that I could leave home as soon as possible. My mother was—and still is—emotionally and physically abusive, and the sooner I could escape, the better.

I joined the Marine Corps at seventeen and had discipline problems. I was soon after diagnosed with Borderline Personality Disorder (which is highly heritable), another reason why I wanted to avoid parenthood. I met my husband in the Marines, and after I was discharged, we married. I had a pregnancy scare and miscarriage early in our relationship, which contributed greatly to my fear of pregnancy and repugnance for giving birth. My husband and I agreed early in the relationship that if either of us changed our minds about having kids, then it would be a deal-breaker, and we'd terminate the marriage. He had a vasectomy a year ago.

Jessica Blom, 29
Happy ChildFree Housewife
Colorado

"Why don't you want kids?" This is a question I've been asked since I married my husband seven years ago. Many people assume it's because of my poor health that I've decided not to add to the population (I don't bother to correct them). The reality is that I made this decision at the ripe ol' age of five. At the time I had had little or no contact with babies. I was, and still am, an only child who enjoyed her alone and quiet time. I never had a baby-doll. I preferred to play with My Little Ponies and Barbie. Loved Tinker Toys and Legos. Life was nice, quiet, and normal. So when my mother signed up to be part of a babysitting co-op, I was rather surprised when a woman came to our house and left her four- to six-month-old with us. I was pretty sure it was an alien. E.T. was in my house and I had no Reese's.

To my five year old brain this small pink thing provided an interesting way to pass the time. And apparently they didn't eat Reese's, they drank milk. I followed my Mom around the house while she fed, burped, and put the infant down to sleep. Wholly uninteresting at this point. That is, until it opened its mouth and emitted the most horrible racket I had ever heard. It was terrible! Wailing and carrying on like someone had stolen its favorite toy. When was the Mothership going to come beam this thing back up?! Finally my mom was able to quiet the miserable sounds and the baby drifted off. I looked at my mom and asked, "Was I this terrible?" Mom explained that I had my moments as an infant. I distinctly remember telling her ," I never want one." I left the room and refused to be near the child after that. I'm almost thirty now and happily Child Free.

Clarice Bourgeois, 29

Public Relations

Berlin, Germany

When I was twelve, and up till my late teens, I knew I was going to have kids. I wanted five boys and two girls—two of the boys would be twins. I wanted a pack of kids, because large families seemed to be closer. Most of my friends had two or three siblings, and two of them had seven kids! There was always someone at home to feed them or help them with their homework, or simply play. I only have a brother, and we never really bonded. I guess I wanted to make up for that. I wanted someone to have my back. I wanted my own "human beings" to help me feel secure and loved. We'd all travel together and I'd teach them several languages and take them to hear my favorite bands. They would be people I'd love to hang out with.

I was going to have kids. Because, why not?

Then something terrible happened: I grew up. Yes. I just grew up. While in high school, I noticed that these friends spent their evenings in the library because they couldn't study at home. They didn't have their own space, or it was too noisy for them to concentrate. Others couldn't join us on exchange trips to the UK or Spain, because their parents couldn't afford to pay for all their kids. So to be fair, none of them got to go.

I made it to university. It was hard because I was struggling financially, working full-time during the holidays to pay my bills and afford rent and textbooks. My mother did the best she could, but she couldn't help much. The same kids who couldn't afford to go on field trips in high school where now richer than me. Some of them never bothered to find work. They didn't need to. In France, scholarships are not awarded on the basis of grades. They take into account your parents' salaries and other social factors such as how many other siblings your parents must raise. My childhood friend who was one of seven siblings never had to worry about paying his bills. Why was he rewarded? Just for being *born* into a large family? I felt bad for being jealous of him and thinking it was so unfair.

Then I had to find a job, to relocate, to start a grown-up life. I didn't think about having kids for years. It was just not on the agenda. I have changed jobs, cities and countries several times in the past decade. I needed to find the right place for me, where I would eventually feel at home. So here I am, in Berlin. I have a job, a cute little flat, friends, pets, and a nice social life. So now I hear, "All you need is a baby!"

Over the past few years I have actually thought about it. Most of my friends got engaged, married, had kids. Do I want that?

I look at their pictures on Facebook. *Aww, this is a cute baby!* But would I want one? No. I don't want children. First, I don't think I'll ever trust anyone enough to have a child with him. My mother got married twice, and she is twice a widow. I miss having a dad, and I can't imagine raising a child on my own. Yes, this is an extreme case, BUT it can happen.

Then, I would never have a child as long as I can't offer what is best for him. I do have a job, as does my boyfriend, but would that be enough? No. Not enough to pay for a good school, good medical care, school field trips, cultural expeditions with his parents ... When I said as much to my friends, they replied, "A child only needs his parents love to be happy." Oh, really? Remember when you were six and everyone but you had this cool toy or those awesome trainers? Did you feel contented at break time, because you knew your parents loved you? I don't think so. We take our parents' love for granted. Did you remember the kids who got to go on great days out with their families, or even holidays abroad? God know I was jealous of that kid called Sylvain, whose parents always (always!) took him abroad. He visited the pyramids in Egypt and the Parthenon in Athens ... I was already attracted to such things, so even with all the love my mom gave me, I wished I could go on those amazing trips instead of sitting around in my garden all summer long.

I don't want my kids to be frustrated like I was. I don't want my kids to spend all their holidays working to go to university. In response to this argument, a Brazilian friend of mine said, "But you're European! It's so easy for you guys to get scholarships! Look, we had trouble finding a kindergarten for Mia, but because her mother is French, we got a scholarship to send her to the French kindergarten, and we hardly have to pay anything!" Well, I'm happy for Mia. She's going to have fun, but thanks to the French government, not her parents. If I had a child, I would want to raise it by myself, with my own money. I think that once you decide to have your child, it is your responsibility to care for him. Everyone can go through a rough patch and get the help they need, but having a baby when you don't really know how you'll afford it is wrong. Your children should not be a burden on your country's economy.

Many people label me as "damaged" when I explain that I don't want a child mostly for financial reasons. I know that there would be a good chance my child could end up unemployed, even if he got several degrees. "Just because it was hard for you doesn't mean it will be the same for your kids," they say. Okay, maybe. But you can't deny other truths, such as that we live on an overpopulated Earth that will soon run out of resources. Having more and more children ruins the ecosystem. "You're just being paranoid," they reply. I'm not paranoid. Thinking about the world you live in, understanding its rules and risks is something everyone should do, for our own good. For our own future.

I'm not selfish, either, as people like me are often labeled. How is it selfish to think of someone else's best interests? Yes, in this case, this person, my potential child, is unborn. And it will be remain that way. To me, breeders are selfish. Parents and parents-to-be act like *their* kids are not part of the problem. You know that old saying, "You're not stuck in traffic, you ARE traffic"? Well, that is what I'd like to tell parents and people who want a child whenever they complain about the rates of unemployment, how expensive everything is (education, etc.) and how sad it is that the Planet is being ruined (I still don't understand how "green" people can say they respect the environment when they have children, which, by the way, is the most polluting thing you can ever do). After all, people who don't want kids are helping to further a bigger cause. We contribute to the soothing of this planet, of our countries' economies. We took time to think about ourselves and our own needs, and we were brave enough to realize that having kids is too important to be done lightly and can't be justified by excuses such as "maternal instinct."

"You're still young," they say. "In five years you'll have changed your mind." I'm turning thirty in three months. Is twenty-nine really too young? If I said I wanted kids, would people tell me the same thing—that I am too young to make such a decision? I'm tired of all these assumptions. I'm tired of the fact that my not wanting kids makes me—in other people's minds— selfish, sad, pessimistic and paranoid, or someone who hasn't "found the right way."

This is not true. I'm okay as I am. I have found balance in my life. I don't need to create my own human beings anymore. I've grown up; I've matured. And I wish everyone would accept the fact that a woman doesn't need to have children to feel morally and socially accomplished. After all, I'm part of the team who's preserving our world.

Erin Mentzer, 29

Deputy Clerk

Frankfort, Kentucky

I'm a Yankee transplant living in Frankfort, Kentucky, and I'm content with my childfree life. While some make the decision not to have children at a particular point, I grew up simply never desiring them. I preferred plush animals to baby dolls, and I never played with toys such as pretend kitchens and vacuum cleaners (which may explain why I have a cluttered house and dislike cooking). At a young age, I spent lots of time with my little brother and male neighbors. In adulthood, I've shed most of my tomboy ways, but a lot of feminine proclivities still mystify me, including the fear of the biological clock that so many women hear ticking. While other girls dreamed of big weddings and lots of babies, I dreamed about a silent, cozy house with a couple of cats and lots of books.

Before I met my now-husband, I assumed I would marry someone I had met in high school or college and have children. That's what is expected and I didn't question it. Even then, my boyfriend and I agreed that I would work and he would be a stay-at-home dad. That should have been a dead giveaway that I was not cut out for motherhood! College came and went and I never did marry any of my sweethearts. Then I met Lin, an older divorced commercial driver—a father who had a vasectomy after his third son was born. We unexpectedly fell in love, and a year later, I moved to Kentucky to be with him. He made it clear early on that he had no intention of having more children. I cannot say that I wrestled with this stipulation, but it did weigh on my mind sometimes—at least when people asked if we were planning on having children. I decided that I loved Lin so much that I was willing to forgo parenthood to be with him. We ended up getting married in a chalet surrounded by loved ones. I have no regrets.

My career has further cemented my childfree beliefs. Since 2008, I have worked for the justice system as a deputy clerk for family court in the county courthouse. I handle all the paperwork and cases for child support, terminations of parental rights, adoptions, and dependency/neglect/abuse courts. In addition to my office work, I serve as a bench clerk, seated next to the judge in court and writing down his rulings on docket sheets. I have a front seat at the drama of people's lives. Everyone I see is a parent. It astounds me how many broken couples use their children as weapons, how many mothers and fathers who once were in love now scream at each other over child support money. I see deserving parents ruled against because the other parent had money for an attorney. Worse yet, I see men and women who thought like I did when I was younger—who didn't know that parenthood is a choice, not a requirement, and had children because it's the way of things, not because they wanted them. I have cases where parents have clearly abandoned their children—either by falling into drugs, or by leaving with no care of what would happen to their offspring. The children become wards to the state and sometimes repeat the mistakes of their parents, ending up in juvenile court and eventually criminal court if they never reform. It's a sad cycle to watch and it makes me wonder what kind of parent I would have been. But since I will never have children, I don't need to worry. Also, from watching these cases, I see how big a job parenthood is. It doesn't seem like something I have the patience to do! Thankfully, I had a happy childhood with two parents who loved each other. I honestly have the best mother ever and I don't think I could ever live up to that. I really admire her for all she did for me and my brother. I see people whose children don't appreciate them at all. Having children is no guarantee of lifelong devotion and unconditional love.

One of my biggest passions is community theater. I like entertaining people and I like going to shows, too. I've been fortunate to land both big and small roles and I have the flexibility that every director loves. I find that most of my cast mates are college-aged or retired with adult children. It's very rare to see parents in the theater world. I have friends who tell me about the exciting things they used to do—until they had kids. I've even known people to say stuff like, "I'd like to (insert fun hobby here) for one more year before I hang up the towel and have kids." I don't want time-frames and deadlines. I want to grab life and enjoy the hell out of it.

I'm a very busy person with a rich, fulfilling life. I'm able to head out of the house on a whim. I don't need to find a babysitter whenever I want to do anything. I have the free time to help others when they need it. My husband and I can let friends and family live with us without worrying about how the kids will react (we currently have a theater friend and my brother-in-law living in our home). We don't have to worry about school districts and teachers and arranging play-dates. I can ride airplanes and go to fancy restaurants with no fear of disrupting my fellow passengers or diners. I don't have to miss work whenever a child gets sick. I can join organizations and not worry about fitting meetings around a child's schedule. I can choose to make meal plans for the week or I can choose to eat a big bowl of ice cream for dinner. No one will call me a "bad mommy" if I want to enjoy alcoholic beverages in a bar or the privacy of my home. And that week-long trip to the Netherlands I am taking in the spring with a friend? That would never happen if I had children. I am a worrier. I wouldn't be able to leave them behind and I wouldn't be able to afford to take them with me, either. Children would squelch these kind of opportunities. Parents might argue that having children is rewarding and that they don't mind sacrificing their freedom. I respect that mindset; I prefer that parents devote their lives to their offspring and help guide them and teach them to be good human beings. It's just not what I want for myself.

In the religious satire *Saved*, the protagonist Mary says, "Why would God make us all so different if he wanted us to be the same?" I agree. Some of us were created to be parents and some of us not. I have my own special ways of contributing to society, from acting to doing volunteer work to offering a listening ear. I rejoice that people are so unique, celebrate our differences and treasure the ways we can help each other, parents or not.

Thirties

Iriny Samy, 30

English Teacher / Aerobics Instructor

Cairo, Egypt

I've been married for four and a half years. At age sixteen I decided to stay childfree. I was impatient around kids and I used to pity mothers and worry that I'd be that kind of woman one day. Their lives really sucked. When I got engaged I had nightmares about becoming pregnant and having a baby and would wake up so depressed that I decided to speak frankly with my fiancé; he would have to choose me or a family and kids. He (and many others) thought I would change my mind, so he just said okay, that we would think about it again in four years. I said "I won't change my mind," but he just smiled. After almost five years, he has begun looking at kids in a different way—as if they are angels—but I still see them constraining my inner me.

I think most people know why childfree people don't want to have kids—too much responsibility, too tiring, they don't feel nurturing, don't like kids, are too impatient, are already satisfied and happy with their lives, can find no logical reason to, believe the world is already too full of pain and suffering, and they are freaked out by all the bad parenting they see every day (and have experienced in their own lives). To someone like me, having children seems crazy.

In other words, I am happy to be free and think that being traditional is stupid. Yes, people do not approve, but it's my life and if I had listened to them, I wouldn't have accomplished so much. The reason I have been able to fulfill most of my dreams is that I don't have children. To those who think we are crazy, I say, remember that it's a personal issue. Let us be different, let us exercise free will, and please do not be disrespectful by challenging our right to choose our own paths.

It's better to ruin your carpet than ruin your life, and my Labrador is my life.

Connie, 30
Accountant
San Antonio, Texas

Looking back at my childhood, I realize I never thought about being a mother. I always drew pictures of myself in a business suit and traveling while my classmates drew pictures of families and children.

When I started dating seriously in my mid-twenties, men who were interested in having families scared me. I was even engaged to someone like that, but I couldn't tell him. In the end I ended the engagement a few days before the wedding. A month later I started dating my now husband. People thought it was too soon, but my heart was already out of the relationship before officially breaking it off. My husband and I wanted the same things in life, and six months later we were engaged. We married three months later. We have been married five years and it just gets better. We call our dog our "fur-child" and love our life the way it is. My husband got a vasectomy close to our third wedding anniversary.

I'm glad to have a choice. In the past women didn't have much of a say. I encourage other men and women to follow their "gut." Don't succumb to peer pressure, and find support with other childfree/childless friends.

Anonymous, 31
Property Management
Maine

I am the youngest of twelve. My father is one of nine children. Thus far, my siblings have produced sixteen offspring, with more on the way. Growing up, I was acutely aware of the strain of too many kids on limited resources. Twelve was too many. There wasn't enough beds, enough clothes, enough food, and not enough love to go around. My parents both worked two jobs, and still there was never enough. In a house with so many bodies, so much need, daily existence was about survival. About fighting to

112

make sure you could get as much of what you needed as you could. You knew it would never be enough. Four of us were sexually abused because no one was protecting us. Only one of us graduated from college, because there wasn't enough money. We were very poor, and half of us were not able to break the cycle of poverty.

So one day, when I was twenty, I decided I'd had enough. I chose not to have a child that I couldn't provide for or love. I decided to break the cycle of poverty, and that meant not having a child. I've spent the last eleven years of my life healing from my childhood experiences. I have subsequently been afforded the opportunity to grow into the best version of myself. I've had a chance to learn strength, persistence, appreciation and best of all, patience. I've been lucky enough to find and marry my best friend, and we are unapologetically child free.

Anonymous, 31
Government Worker
Baytown, Texas

There are four major reasons why I have chosen not to procreate:

My childhood. I can already hear the whispering. No; I haven't gotten "over it." It was the unspoken fact that I was a burden, the reason why Mom and Dad couldn't really have all that they desired. They had to make sacrifices for ME, and it was MY fault, a guilt that I was well aware of and sentenced to carry as long as I lived under their roof. And I'd better show gratitude 24/7. If not, there would be consequences. I was privileged and better "damn well" know it. I was verbally abused and mistreated by both of my parents. I was just "there"—a product of my parents' physical activity. The spotlight was reserved for those my parents thought deserved it, like my sister. She was the accomplished "star" of the family—spectacular, intelligent, worthy. Only I knew better. This wolf in sheep's clothing was a master of disguise. I knew what she was and the things she did. I was never a priority, more of an afterthought. For years, I begged my parents to pay attention to me; I even acted out to try and get their attention. Their response was to reprimand me and tell me that I was a moron, that I'd end up pregnant and disgrace the family name. So, now I choose to live my life as I want to, devoting time to myself, however I please. I have given myself back the attention I never had ... I created my OWN spotlight. I am center stage!! I am the accomplished college graduate, the "prettier" sibling, the fashionista ... the star the family *just knew I would be ...*"

My husband's childhood was very similar to mine, only he was raised by a single mother. He went through some of the same torment as I did, verbally abused and mistreated, things that would crush any child's self-esteem. He was raised poor and now chooses to give himself ALL (love, time, affection) of the things he never had as a child.

I refuse to be defined as a Bitch. (Strong words meant for emphasis.) My "role" as a woman as defined by the Baptist Church was to lie down and bear children. For as long as I can remember, I have been groomed to accept my role as a woman. Every Sunday and multiple times a week, I was surrounded by examples of what I should become: a deaconess' wife, a reverend's wife, a pastor's wife. I was created to be suppressed and dominated by a man. I would be obedient, serve my husband, and breed.

My role models of motherhood were not positive. I witnessed ALL that my sister went through as a single mother at the age of eighteen. And that was far enough! I will never forget the screaming matches between my parents and my sister, the battles between my sister and her "baby daddy," and the look on my father's face of sheer disgust and disappointment. My mother was NEVER happy. During my childhood, I witnessed and suffered her fury, confusion, and depression, as she changed from active mother to recluse ... I grew tired of her relentless venting toward me and at me. If this is what motherhood was, I wanted NO part of it!

My husband and I have so many freedoms we are unwilling to give up. We are childfree and love it! We love to travel, we love the nightlife, we love being able to do WHATEVER we want, WHENEVER we want. People argue that children don't stop them from doing what they choose, but I strongly disagree. We can decide at the spur of the moment to travel out of town or take a cruise. We often don't get home until three or even four o'clock in the morning. You don't have that type of flexibility with a kid!

Paulinha Pimentel, 31
Attorney
Salvador, Bahia, Brazil

When I was a teenager, getting pregnant was my worst nightmare. My family was always saying things like, "If you get pregnant, your life will be over. You'll have to stop everything to take care of your baby." Also, I was scared to death of anything or anyone that might get in the way of what I wanted. As a teenager, I wanted to be a famous dancer, artist, model, and so on. I was always trying things, having fun and learning, never wanting anything to stop me ... and that's what having a kid would mean. But I guess it's like that for all teens.

While I was in my twenties, friends got pregnant. I started to wonder about this more seriously. I saw them, their lives, their reactions—their fear, their needs and their despair. I saw all the good and bad things. Actually, I saw more bad than good and began to wonder, why have kids?

Some say you must have kids before thirty, and I think, how is that? Those friends could not finish university, couldn't have their own houses, had to live (along with their husbands and baby) with their parents, were forced to listen to whatever their parents or in-laws wanted to say. It's never a good choice. They had to depend on others and abandon their plans, studies and work.

When I was about twenty-five, everyone finished university and started thinking about marriage and families. I was still trying to find a good reason to have kids. I always suspected that the sacrifice is immense, that you must give up everything for the kid. Well, it's an option, but I don't see many happy faces. I guess people don't think about it; they just go ahead because that's life. They do what is expected—no questioning, no reasoning. It's not really my style to do things without asking why.

The rewards of procreation are never proportionate to the sacrifice, and most people want kids because they're cute and they have your blood. Then they realize how much responsibility they've taken on—especially women, who have to work so hard, take care of the house, the kids, worry about how they are doing in school, have to take care of themselves and their husbands. It's too much to strive to be a good mother, good wife, good worker, good friend and take care of one's self; it's just too much! Very few can handle it. They keep smiling, saying it is wonderful to be a mama, but if you look closely, they are collapsing, they have no time. Trying to do it all is too much stress.

Having kids was good in the past when you could stay home, devote the day to them—no hurry, no worries. On the other hand, kids didn't make women happy, because they were stuck at home all day, bored, while their husbands were working. Today it is a nightmare. Some just give up sleeping. Sex is an event. All this ruins lives—a family, a marriage.

Also, there are so many children alone in the world who need someone to take care of them, give some love and assistance, a place to call home. Isn't it selfish to bring kids into the world knowing there are already so many helpless children praying every night for a home?

There are seven billion people in the world, and this number is increasing. How long will our planet support so many? Times have changed and people must open their eyes. Surviving is no longer about multiplying, it's about choosing not to.

Having kids is no guarantee that you won't be alone when you are old. Kids can die, can be born with some problem that means you will have to take care of them forever. They may hate you. There are so many factors you can't count on. Most people think that won't happen to them. There are no guarantees. It's better to count on yourself, work hard, study hard enough not to have to depend on anyone when you are old.

Stéphanie Lafleur, 31
Public Servant
Ottawa, Ontario

I was twenty-five years old when I first realized I did not want children. The topic had never come up in my previous relationships; therefore, I hadn't given it much thought. While I was filling out a questionnaire on a dating website, I surprised myself by automatically answering "no" to the question, "Do you want children?" But then, the more I thought about it, the more certain I was that it was the right answer.

As a child and teenager I was extremely timid. I was scared of becoming an adult and scared of the many choices and experiences that lay ahead. It seemed that life was much more difficult for me than for others. At twenty-five, I was happy with what I had managed to accomplish, despite my shyness. I had a university degree, an apartment in the city, and a great job. I was learning to overcome my fears and I was finally in charge of my life. Having children would mean taking a step back and making someone else a priority and I wasn't willing to do that. It had taken me so long to pursue my own dreams, and I was just getting started.

On that dating website I met my husband-to-be, who also shared my views about parenthood. We are more than happy with our choice. Some people call it selfishness, but we prefer to call it self-awareness. We don't doubt that there is much joy involved in raising children, and we greatly respect those who decide to become parents. But we remain true to what we feel is right for us, as we continue to make our own happiness a priority.

Rebeccah, 32

Head Start Preschool Teacher
Denver, Colorado

For me the decision to be child-free was driven by an accumulation of factors over time, rather than one or two major incidents. I can't remember how old I was exactly when I made the choice, but I would guess I was in my teens, around thirteen or fourteen. There were three strong reasons.

To begin with, all I ever heard growing up from most of the adults around me was how hard it was to raise children. I had the impression that nothing was worse. Everything from "I was so sick when I was pregnant," to, "Oh, I was in labor for thirty hours and it was the most painful thing I've ever been through," to, "Children are so expensive," to, "My husband and I barely have any time for ourselves." Even when I was a young child, before I consciously knew that I didn't want children, something about the whole process did not seem quite right to me. I didn't want any of that, especially the part where I wouldn't have any time for myself. As I got older, I was relieved to find out that having kids was actually optional.

The second reason is that I've been working with children off and on for twenty-plus years, if you count babysitting. I didn't make my choice to be child-free because I don't like kids; I've worked with almost every kind of child there is. The other side of that coin, though, is that I've observed first-hand what it takes to properly raise a child … and it's a *lot*. More than what I care to take on. Raising a typical child involves all sorts of trials and tribulations. Potty training, for example. Even the best kids will test and test their parents' boundaries, patience, and tempers. In that I'm certified as a special educator, I see what it takes to raise a child with special needs, and there is always a chance you'll have one of those. Not only does raising such a child involve the aforementioned delights of child-rearing, but the additional possibility of occupational therapy, physical therapy, speech therapy, behavioral therapy, medication, speech augmentation devices, wheelchairs, and the like. I commend parents of special needs children; I know myself well enough to realize I couldn't do it. They're better people than I, that's for sure. My job is just to help. Because I sometimes work twelve hour days, if I did have a family, I would be spending more time with other people's children than my own.

The third reason is that as I've grown, I've learned that I like to do lots of other things more than picking up kids from daycare, fixing dinner, and lying around on the couch all evening. I've always enjoyed traveling, and being child-free offers me the time and money to go on a few vacations a year—vacations where I don't have to worry about gate-checking a stroller and a Pack 'n Play. I now compete in Triathlons—something I never thought I could do. I gave myself a year and a half to go from couch potato to participating in my first triathlon. If I had a child, I never could have committed so many hours to the training, which has been important to my physical and mental well-being. I've participated in three triathlons.

Every day I am reminded of why I decided not to have children. Whenever one of my preschool parents complains about how hard raising children is, or my kids misbehave, or I need to hit the gym to shake off a bad day, I always take a minute to appreciate my decision to stay child-free.

Rebecca Jackson, 32
Internal Communications
Melbourne, Australia

The first firm realization that I do not want children came the night of my wedding. Late in the evening, as everyone was exiting the building, I received my first "When are you having a baby?" query. My answer was polite and short: "We have no plans." Little did I know how often I would be repeating it. The queries became frequent and thus prevalent in my thoughts and discussions between my husband and me. While he remained ambivalent, I became hardened in my resolve. The more people asked, the more reasons I came up with. I was shocked at some of the people who assumed I'd be ready to drop everything to make babies. I thought they knew me better.

I am the eldest of six children and one of the older grandchildren in my family. This probably sounds like the perfect preparation for parenthood, but although I have always been around children and caring for them, I wouldn't have interacted with them—given a choice. I don't hate children, but seeing a cute baby doesn't cause any stirrings of maternal longing in my ovaries.

I have a few key reasons for not wanting children. I have a career, I just finished studying and have reclaimed my life, and I want to travel and experience things with my husband and friends; children do not fit into this picture. Furthermore, I don't think I would make a particularly good parent. I can barely care for a plant or a pet, let alone a little person. Finally, there are enough people on the planet. No need for me to make a new one.

I think I have been pretty lucky. My friends and family are accepting (or in quiet denial) about my choice. I don't think everyone should stop making babies, but I do think people should accept the choice not to have children as an informed one—important and not to be taken lightly. For now and the foreseeable future, I am happily childfree, and I voice my reasoning through my blog, "Reasons I Should Not Breed" (Acetonescribe.wordpress.com).

Jessica Copeland Sparks, 32
Military Wife
Dongducheon, South Korea

I was the only child in a two-parent household. My parents divorced when I was in my mid twenties. I have a BS in Animal Science and was a Veterinary Technician for almost seven years. I have been married for two years, to a United States soldier.

By the time I was in high school I knew that 2.5 children, suburbs and a white picket fence were just not for me. Also, my mother raised me not to get married and have children until my education was complete and I was able to make a life for myself.

I believe my life is happier without children. I have the ability to sleep when I need to, wake when I want and eat what, when and where I choose. I always find it entertaining to hear parents complain about their children then follow up their complaints by proclaiming how fulfilling their lives are. I have yet to meet a parent who does not have an almost daily story about how their child has "stressed" them in some way. If there was any other issue in your life causing you that much stress, people would be lining up to tell you to remove said stress. Somehow parents want to encourage you to join their faction. Misery loves company, perhaps?

All evidence to the contrary, parents insist that having children is the best thing that could ever happen. I choose to just say no. I have a husband who is the love of my life, the man of my dreams, my best friend and every other cliché I can think of. I do not see how anything that interferes with that bond could be healthy or fulfilling.

My family understands and supports my decision. Several family members have chosen to be child free as well. I tend to surround myself with child-free friends, so obviously they support me. That said, being in the "military family," I get a completely different reaction. Not wanting children in the military world is pretty much like having the plague.

The typical reaction I get from people outside my family and circle of friends is dismay and pity. I am from a small Southern town, where you are expected to get married and start breeding directly out of high school. It is pretty much the same reaction I get in the military, where the first question is always "So, do you have children?" Perhaps it is my answer—"No, nor do I want any"—that ostracizes me.

I have never felt pressured to have or not have children. It is my decision, and the one I am most confident about. Other people's opinions are just that. I know who I am and what I want in life, and having children, without a doubt, does not fit into that equation.

Living the military life I am surrounded by children, and none of the parents seem happy. Do they complain? Daily. If not complaining about their children directly, they are complaining about what their husbands have or have not done, for or with the child.

I do not particularly care for children, nor do I care to be around them. The younger they are, the less I am inclined to interact with them. I do not find babies adorable. I also do not believe that children are a miracle, when upwards of 50,000 are born every day.

J.R., 32

Cosmetologist

Orlando, Florida

I knew from a very young age that I did not want to have children.

I was six or seven years old when I told my family. They of course laughed at me, but now they accept and support my decision. As a little girl, I didn't daydream of Mr. Right and children's names. I was more concerned about finding a career that I would enjoy, owning a house, and rescuing animals.

I chose not to procreate because I do not enjoy being around children in the slightest. My list of reasons has become quite long; for me there is not one good one.

I am extremely happy with my decision to remain child-free. I would not have had the opportunities that I have had—changing careers (a few times), traveling, and living in several states—if I'd had children. Of course people throughout the years have told me, "You will change your mind one day." But that day never came, and it never will.

This is my life, my choice, and I am happy.

Lindsay Aronstein, 32

Business Owner, Women's Clothing

Houston, Texas

I own a women's clothing store in Houston, Texas. My husband and I have been married for almost seven years and have three wonderful fur kids (dogs). When we first got married, we naturally thought we would have children; however, things didn't go as planned. Since we had waited a few years before trying, we witnessed our friends having babies and all the stress that goes along with that. We tried for a while, but soon realized that we would have to undergo IVF. Once the doctor told us the plan, we made up our minds that it was not what either of us really wanted. The next day we took a trip to Colorado and reflected over all the wonderful things we could do together since we were not having children. We were relieved and realized that we never really wanted kids to begin with; we just thought it was what we were supposed to do. Mostly we worried about what our parents would think, but they were more than supportive. In the beginning friends would ask "Why not adoption?" while others silently envied us. Our choice not to have children has had a positive impact on our marriage. We travel whenever we want and as a family of two, we have zero stress about planning our future.

Jenny Johnke-Bean, 33
Retail
Gilroy, California

I think I was born knowing I never wanted kids. While most girls were dreaming of the day they would marry and have children, I could have cared less. When I was a little girl, I had an image of myself as a successful business lady with a boyfriend, living life to the fullest without kids. Pretty much a *Sex and the City* character in the making. Although not wanting kids felt natural even at that early age, I didn't tell anyone because I knew I would get the same, "Oh, you'll change your mind when you're older," crap. I am married now, but I still don't want children.

I never even babysat! I preferred to hang out with kids older as well. I remember going to parties at my parents' friends' houses where some of the kids were *so* annoying that they exhausted me. I'd try to hide, but somehow they found me. It's not that I hated kids; I just couldn't understand them. I couldn't *wait* to be older and live the fabulous life I'd always dreamed about.

Being an only child, I also relied more on myself and focused on what made me happy. I was told I was selfish. I'd be lying if I said I never fantasized about having kids, but as I got older I realized it was only a fantasy. Reality slapped me in the face when I was nine years old and started having terrible and debilitating panic attacks that still haunt me to this day. The thought of having to take care of another living being sent my heart racing. I actually have a fear that one day I will wake up and want children, but the last thing I wish is to be is a hypocrite. Then again, I am being quoted in a book, so I think I've pretty much made up my mind. Perhaps in another lifetime I will have children. At least in this one I can say I was true to my word.

Liz Taylor, 33
Veterinary Technician
Pittsburgh, Pennsylvania

My decision to be childfree was not made lightly. In the beginning, it was not necessarily conscious. I couldn't imagine being a mother. Once the subject of kids or no kids officially came up, I did a lot of serious thinking about the ways my life would change, and I just didn't want the responsibility of properly raising a productive member of society. I didn't want the financial burden. I didn't want to be sleep-deprived for the next two decades. I didn't want to change my lifestyle, because I rather enjoy things just the way they are. In my pros and cons list, the cons far outweighed the pros. I was not going to have a child just because that is what I was "supposed" to do. I know myself well enough to realize that motherhood would not be a good fit—not because I'm selfish or immature, or any of those other things that childfree people hear when making their decision known. I don't think anyone can ever be fully prepared to be a parent, but I do feel that there are a lot of people who don't put nearly enough thought into the decision and end up disappointed. Creating a child and then devoting your life to preparing that child to become a responsible, moral, upstanding citizen is an enormous responsibility. In my experience, a lot of my friends who want kids or already have kids could not see past the cute, cuddly, snuggly baby all wrapped up in a perfect bundle. It seems that a lot of people love the idea of having a baby but feel let down that parenthood doesn't quite turn out the way it is often portrayed in the movies or on television. It is a lot of hard work, often full of frustration and disappointment. I am sure that it is also rewarding in many ways that I don't understand, but I honestly don't feel that I am missing out. I feel rewarded in countless other ways.

Society definitely pressures women (and men) to have kids. Because I am a woman, they assume I spend my days wishing for motherhood. When people find out that I do not have any desire to be a mother, they view me as an oddity or assume there's "something wrong" with me, physically or psychologically. My bigger issue with society is that people like me, who don't have the desire to procreate, are excluded. The assumption and expectation is that all "natural" and "normal" women want to have babies. In my experience, any variance from what is considered a normal step in the checklist of life is not viewed positively.

I don't recall exactly when I decided that I definitely did not want children. I do remember that even as a kid, when I would play with my dolls, I rarely played "house" with them. I was more interested in playing beauty shop—painting their faces and cutting their hair. As I got older, I never fantasized about being a mom. I did dream of getting married someday. When my (now) husband and I started dating, it didn't take long before the subject came up. Thankfully, he is on the same page about being childfree. Like me, he has never wanted children, and after nearly twelve years of marriage, we are more certain than ever that our decision was right for us.

Without the financial constraints and endless worries that having kids brings, I feel a great sense of freedom to do all sorts of things in life. I know quite a few people who had a big checklist of things to do before they had kids. They had to scramble to cross those things off the list so they could have their kids. I don't want to have to hurry through anything. I don't want to put my dreams and goals on hold. I am quite happy that I have a lifestyle that is flexible. I truly enjoy being an adult, childfree woman.

Melissa Owen, 34

Make-Up Artist

Newcastle, New South Wales

My inspiration for writing this essay was an article I read in a national magazine. It compared three families—one with two children, one with none and one with four. I was fine with the article until I read this comment by one of the mothers: "People who choose not to have children are missing out." Even as I write these words, my blood is boiling!

How am I missing out, exactly? A horrendous childbirth, a vagina that will never be the same, a child who needs constant care, attention and financial assistance, no time to spend with my husband, having to listen to whining about the littlest things …. The list goes on and on. When I tell people that I have no interest in becoming a mother, they tilt their heads and say, "Oh, you will change your mind."

Some see my husband and me as weird or unusual for not wanting children. Well, if liking my life the way it is and enjoying being my own person makes me weird then I guess I am.

I was never one of those children who would talk about how many kids they were going to have. I loved my dolls and had many, but I never felt I would one day have my own baby. While my playmates would talk about the names they would pick for their children it never crossed my mind. I would talk about meeting my fairytale prince and getting married, living happily-ever-after, but having children was not part of that.

My birth father made it clear that he had never wanted children and that my mum had talked him into having me, so I was made to feel like a burden. He was a committed Jehovah's Witness. When I was born I was jaundiced and needed a blood transfusion. Jehovah's Witnesses do not believe in blood transfusions, so he wanted the doctors to let me die. My mum was hysterical, so my grandmother stepped in and I was made a ward of the state. It was my grandmother who gave the doctors permission to save me. I was first told this story when I was around eight years old. It broke my heart that this man I idolized hadn't wanted me at all. He really enjoyed telling me that Santa Claus wasn't real and that the Easter Bunny didn't exist; I was only four at the time. Needless to say, he is no longer a part of my life.

Having a father who treated me like an unwanted puppy probably played a big part in my decision to remain childless. I do not want to sacrifice for a child; I just want to live my life for me and enjoy the things I love. Some people will say I am selfish, but this is my life, isn't it?

For twelve years I was an only child; then my mum and stepdad had my little sister and another sister two years later. Both my parents worked long hours in their business and I was the only one who could look after my sisters while they were at work. I cooked for my sisters, bathed them, fed them, picked them up from school, dressed them, and so on, until my parents arrived home each day. I was like a mini mum. I didn't mind all that much because I love my sisters and my family and I understood that I had to be responsible and reliable. I received an allowance for my work, which meant I could buy the things I wanted. Now I feel that I have already been a mum. Looking after children is the hardest job on earth, and I don't feel the slightest need to do it. Some people think I must hate children, but that's not true at all. I think some kids are great. I was even a teacher for a few years.

I feel in my heart you should only have children if you really want them—not because society says it's your job. I don't judge other women for choosing to have children, but people seem to think it's okay to judge me. I am happy with my life and never feel I'm missing out because I don't have a baby on my hip.

Danielle, 34

Administrator

Auckland, New Zealand

I was raised in a very unhappy household where marriage and children were touted as the ultimate goals in life. When I went to university, I met a guy and very nearly went down that path. I was eager to create the "happy family life" I had been sold but never had. However, leaving home to go to university gave me the space to think for myself, and I began to question the mindless breeding applauded by society. My concerns were swiftly silenced with "You can't worry about that" or "You'll find a way." Once I examined the serious questions independently without getting caught up in whimsical fantasies or social pressure, it was glaringly obvious that I had been fed a lie. The answers to my questions were not pretty. The fantasy and the reality diverged wildly. I was in my early twenties when this realization occurred.

Around this time, I came across a magazine article about Nicki Defago's book *Childfree and Loving It*, and I was hooked: I read everything I could get my hands on about being childfree by choice, and the more I read, the more certain I felt about my decision. There are so many reasons why I choose to be childfree, and they are all center around deep and complex issues that I have thoroughly examined. People tend to think I'm weird, that I over-think matters. Personally, I am horrified at the usual lack of forethought given to such a momentous decision; after all, any parental shortcomings inevitably have a negative impact on a child.

I have yet to find one good reason to breed. The usual "reasons" people give don't stack up, and they tend to be based on or justified by selfish motives, e.g., what the parent will gain from the experience. I find claims of altruism absolutely ridiculous; people have children purely out of self interest and for the sake of ego gratification. I have a strong interest in psychology, and the damage people unknowingly do to their children just horrifies me. Most people are not fit to be parents, and I'm amazed that we are all expected and encouraged to breed without having to prove our competence.

Creating a new person where there wasn't one before seems so extreme and unnecessary. Another consumer. A mini-me (there's that self-interest again). An extra living, breathing human being—the ultimate extravagance. I cannot understand why anybody would think procreation is a good idea. There are too many of us on the planet; the earth is struggling with our upkeep. We treat each other despicably. Our lives are filled with pain—illness, suffering, death and unfair circumstances. Our priorities are confused. Money rules; material goods trump relationships, open minds and knowledge. We kill each other over religion, sexual orientation, ethnicity, even sports. And all this for the great purpose of ... nothing. There is no point to our existence. Why on earth would I voluntarily subject an innocent person to this bullshit? Furthermore, how could I possibly claim it is selfless to do so? It's like throwing kittens into a fire.

I'm non-conventional—a deep, philosophical thinker who doesn't fit in well. I prefer to sit on the sidelines and observe the madness without being a part of it. If I did that with kids, I'd be a seriously uncool and unfair mother. If I tried to integrate for their sake, I'd be anxiety ridden and stressed out—also not ideal qualities in a mother. I see my choice as responsible—for myself, the planet, and the potential child. I am constantly astounded by the idiocy, arrogance and cruelty in this world. Seriously? I don't want my kids growing up here.

Angela LaFrance, 35

Accountant

Las Vegas, Nevada

My mom says she should have known I'd never have kids. When I was little I loved my stuffed animals and had zero interest in dolls. As long as I can remember—at least since age five or six—I knew I didn't want kids. A few early experiences helped push me in that direction. The first was looking at pictures of childbirth in a book my mom had when she was pregnant with my brother. I remember being completely disgusted! The second was when my brother was being potty trained. Even once he was able to use the toilet, he was constantly yelling, "Mom, come wipe me!" Even at six years old I knew I never wanted to be the person who had to respond to that. When he was a little older, we would have to leave restaurants and stores because he was throwing a tantrum or screaming or climbing all over the shoe racks at JC Penney's. We used to visit my uncle's cabin in northern Michigan every summer and one of everyone's favorite things to do was the nighttime ride to look for deer and bears. My brother decided he was afraid of the part of the ride where there were hills, and so my mom had to stay back at the cabin with him. I was so angry that she had to miss out on the ride because of him. Looking back I realize it probably wasn't a big deal for her, but the concept of having to sacrifice things you enjoyed just because of a child's irrational fear infuriated me.

In my teens to mid-twenties, I had a long list of reasons I didn't want kids—too expensive (I didn't go into debt to go to college so I could take care of kids), too hard to go on vacation or have a social life, and so on. Once I was married to a man who would make a good father and I was more financially secure, I started thinking things like, "Having kids wouldn't be the worst thing in the world. Maybe my career isn't that important to me anyway." My husband was pressuring me to at least consider having kids. For a few brief weeks I felt like maybe this was something I could do, something I might even enjoy. But it didn't take long before I realized that not being horrified at the thought of having kids was a long ways from actually wanting them.

These days, if asked why I don't want kids, I'm happy to reply, "I just don't." The initial confusion on people's faces is kind of entertaining, but once they think about it for a minute most of them accept that answer. If you give them reasons they will try to counter those reasons—but even with unlimited time and money and a nanny and all of the things that make parenting as easy as possible, I still wouldn't change my mind.

Even though that decision ultimately contributed to the end of my marriage, I'm one hundred percent confident that it is right for me. I would be totally suffocated and miserable with children. I need a lot of alone time and "down time" to keep me sane, and the parents I know rarely get either of those things. Over the past few years I've been able to do a lot of really amazing volunteer work (some of it benefitting children) and I never would have had the time or energy to do that with kids of my own. This year I was able to move across the country, something I've wanted to do my entire life. I don't have to worry about uprooting children from their friends, or finding a good school, or doing those things all over again if the move doesn't work out. I can feel excited for my friends who truly love children and parenting, but I don't feel like I'm missing anything. My life is not perfect, but it wouldn't be improved by being a parent, and being childfree gives me a lot more freedom to pursue the things that make me happy.

Tonya Kniest, 35
Accounting Specialist
Sedro Woolley, Washington

I remember being Childfree, at least subconsciously, as early as age seven. In daycare, the babies would cry and I *so* badly wanted them to just shut up. While growing up, I never pictured myself as a mother or had fantasies of what "my child" would be like. I've never been keen on loud, constant noises and chaos, so I can only handle kid-related things in small doses. I enjoy my nieces and nephews, but I also know I can escape when I've had enough. I babysat two of them when I was fourteen and they were six and two; it was the longest, most miserable summer of my life! The thought of being tied to someone for eighteen plus years fills me with an intense and smothering claustrophobia.

Maybe it's just my parents' generation (I'm thirty-five, they're sixty-seven now), but my mom was the one who did the majority of the parenting and housework, in addition to working, while my dad could have hobbies or sit on the couch with his beer in the evenings. I can't imagine a more repulsive lifestyle for myself.

I've always valued my freedom. If I want to go out at midnight to buy a pint of ice cream, I'm free to do so without having to find someone to watch the kids. I don't get calls at work saying my child is sick or in trouble. My favorite thing to tell others when asked about my Childfreedom is, "I have dogs. I can lock them in the kennel for eight hours and leave and no one calls the cops on me."

These are my main reasons for choosing not to procreate. I've connected with others who feel the same way, and hearing their reasons further cements my decision. Alternately, none of the arguments from parents pro-children have been appealing enough to make me even consider changing my mind. I love the life I've chosen!

Joel Gardner, 35

Truck Driver

Lansing, Michigan

I first realized I did not want kids when I got my own car. I would spend time out at the local mall watching people, mainly women. The women I saw pushing strollers never seemed to be too happy and in a generally grumpy mood. The younger couples who were also pushing strollers seemed just as unhappy. I quickly assumed that the main reason for their unhappiness was having to take care of the baby.

Until then I'd never really thought about having a baby myself. I believe my people-watching helped solidify the notion that kids were not for me. When I was nineteen or so I went to talk to a urologist regarding a vasectomy. Naturally I was turned down. Nine to ten years later I tried again and was able to finally get the surgery. Best money I ever spent on myself.

After the time I tried and failed to get my first vasectomy, a girlfriend of mine told me she thought she was prego. THAT freaked me out. I knew I didn't want a scare like that again! I've been fixed for seven years or so now and I have never looked back. Better not to have a kid you thought you wanted than to have a kid you wish you didn't have.

Angela Rosales, 35

Admissions Officer

Phoenix, Arizona

I'm a thirty-five-year old, single, Asian-American professional woman. I'm also childfree. I've never been married and I've never had children. I have no desire to marry and have children ... EVER. I'm from a large family—the eldest of five daughters. My culture has always emphasized traditional values, including the importance of family. And even though my parents followed that path, they never tried to force me to follow suit. Even when I was a child, my parents advised me to focus on going to college and getting a good job, to put off finding a boyfriend until college or after. I listened to my parents. They taught me to be ambitious and always to set goals for myself. Marriage and family were at the bottom of that list of goals. I never aspired to be a wife and mother. What mattered was going to school, being financially stable, and being successful in my chosen career. I also wanted to travel the world and make and meet new friends. Coming from a large family has definitely contributed to my embracing "childfreedom."

My sisters (including a pair of twins) are four, five and one-half, and nine years younger than me—huge gaps. When I turned ten, my mother decided to re-enter the workplace after being a stay-at-home mom. My father was working all the time as well and I became the official caretaker. We were latchkey kids so we weren't getting much supervision. I was only a child! I wanted to focus on being a child but was instead forced to grow up quickly. I have observed how my mother and father parented me and my sisters, and I remember how stressed out they almost always were. They wanted us to stay in school and didn't like us being on summer or winter break. They got angry if one of us came home sick and infected them! If one of my sisters acted up in public, I had to help my parents control and discipline them. If I wanted to go play or hang out with friends, my parents insisted I take my sisters with me.

I didn't like what my parents—or I—had to put up with. I acted more mature than the average child by virtue of being an older sister of sisters. I was more serious, more studious, but less social than most children. When I was in high school, I focused hard on my studies and getting into college at a time when my friends couldn't wait to get married and have children. I think a lot of my peers expected I would marry and have kids someday. Truthfully, I thought about having a boyfriend and even tried to set a goal to be married right out of college and have my first child at twenty-five. But I was also daydreaming about doing a job I loved and making money so I could travel the world. I thought I would eventually marry and have kids, but as time wore on and I went to college, I still didn't feel the overwhelming desire to be a wife and mother.

I started dating at nineteen and loved the idea of having a boyfriend. When I moved out of state to start a new life on my own at twenty-five, I thought a lot about my future. I met a man who would become my first (and so far only!) boyfriend, and I did dream about being married and having his child. However, I was sexually inexperienced and still a virgin when we met and after a couple of intimate sessions, I thought he had impregnated me. I was so terrified that I did not sleep for a whole week. I was so relieved when my period came. I soon realized that I was not ready to be pregnant. I thought I had met the man of my dreams, that we would marry and have kids. Sadly, the relationship did not last long after I made the decision to join the Air Force. I struggled with that decision. Should I continue working a temp job and struggle to get by just so I could stay close to my boyfriend? Or would I take control of my life and pursue something that would make me financially stable and give me better job opportunities?

The military lifestyle sounds stressful but it allowed me to see the world and go back to school. I focused on my job in the military, pursuing my master's degree and also my social life. I wanted to meet people and date. I wanted a long-term relationship. However, many of the social events seemed to focus more on family activities. I felt out of place because I was single and had no children.

A few years ago I started researching childfree activities and groups and met and made many new friends who are in the same situation. It seemed that I could never hang out with my friends who were married and had kids or were single parents. So I sought out other childfree people who had free time. After I met my childfree friends in Phoenix, I started seeking out childfree groups on social networking sites. I joined childfree discussion boards and a childfree mailing list. I had become fully aware of my childfree status and how it helped shape who I am today.

Through the advice of a friend and lots of soul-searching, I decided to undergo a tubal ligation in 2009. My mother had spent her entire thirties pregnant and raising kids, which meant that could happen to me! It was one of the most liberating things I have ever done. Not worrying about pregnancy anymore was a godsend.

I have become very passionate about my childfree status and love being around people who share my views. I no longer have patience when it comes to dealing with children. I observed the hardships my parents endured and now see what my twin sisters are going through. They are always struggling financially and never have free time. Now I understood why BOTH my parents had to work ... Raising children is expensive! I have also observed relatives and friends going through the hardships of marriage, divorce, and child-rearing. I can do without that drama. I'd rather take care of my dog than a child. Also, the world is not safe for children anymore.

America is so pro-natal and child-centric that every woman feels pressured to have kids. My maternal instinct was burned out a long time ago. The Dalai Lama said it best: "People take different roads seeking fulfillment and happiness. Just because they're not on your road doesn't mean they've gotten lost." Just because I chose not to be a wife and mother does not mean I am not fulfilled and happy. I have no regrets and I doubt I ever will. I just want to focus on things that make me feel life is worth living. You don't have to be a parent to experience that. I have many childfree role models, including my mother's two younger sisters who are childfree. Also many celebrities and politicians. I have a wonderful circle of childfree friends and continue to meet more like them.

Ed Love, 36

Screenwriter

Canberra, Australian Capital Territory

My first experiences with young children weren't fun: they were noisy, messy, badly brought-up annoyances. I couldn't wait to see the back of them. They interrupted everybody, and there was no peace to be had around them. My own time as a child confirmed this.

I pondered the reason for having kids. Do I really need to perpetuate my family name or my genes? If I want someone to love, there are plenty of people here already who could use some care.

Later in life, as part of a Silicon Valley startup, I lived with a couple who had toddlers. Everything they did took much longer than expected, and their lives were severely limited by the presence of their children.

At age twenty-five, I had a vasectomy. The doctors had a chat to make sure I knew what I was doing, but there was never any doubt for me. It's one of the best things I ever did. I've never considered changing my mind.

I could rabbit on about saving the world from the population problem, but ultimately, it's a selfish decision, for my own benefit. It's given me far more time and money than having kids would.

I am very comfortable being childfree.

Scheris Schuring, 36

Crisis Manager, Microsoft Corporation

Maple Valley, Washington

I can picture the setting as if it was yesterday, yet it has been over thirty-one years.

Five acres of private land amid hundreds of acres of forests and old logging roads, leading up the Onion Peak, which could be seen from my childhood home. My dad built that beautiful house, covered in traditional coastal cedar shakes, in 1979. We had popular burnt orange carpets, twin sliding glass doors in the family room, an awesome never-ending 4,800 square feet to romp in, with a stone fireplace so heavy its weight eventually caused the home to lean. It was there I overheard the secret whispers of each parent regarding marriage and children.

"Don't ever get married, don't ever have kids, it will ruin your life."

"Don't marry a man like your father."

"Don't end up like your mother."

I heard the message loud and I steered clear.

Around that time, my grandmother told me not to stand in front of the microwave because the radiation would interfere with my ability to have children. Not long after, my mom saw me staring into the microwave as I waited for my food and asked me not to. At the age of five I smiled wryly as I looked around the orange Formica counters that beamed brightly from the sun. I now had the gift of knowledge, which would lead me to a life of freedom and independence. My plan was set in motion. I determined to have a better life than my parents. I walked out of that kitchen knowing that my friend—the orange ceramic frog holding the dish sponge in his mouth—wished me well.

As I grew older, many people told me I would change my mind. It became my own personal mission and I resolved never to forget. The age of twenty-nine still seemed too young and age thirty seemed too old, so my time came and went.

My short bouts of baby fever last no more than a few seconds and only happen when I see a newborn sleeping. It only takes one trip to Wal-Mart to remind me why babies are so cute. I did have a desire to know what pregnancy and labor would be like, but Washington State didn't have a Surrogacy program, so life went on. Surprisingly, my thirty-four year old brother and my twenty-three-year-old sister are also leaning toward the decision not to procreate. It is odd when our parents comment on our decisions without understanding the impact of their actions. They have said they won't accept responsibility for guiding us one way or another.

That's okay; there is no ill will over this matter.

Four years ago I married my sweetheart and inherited a stepdaughter. She never had her biological mother and when I came into her life, she craved a maternal relationship and had fantasized about all the ways she wanted to be mothered. The three of us embraced our religion and my thoughts on motherhood have softened, or maybe one should say strengthened. Last year, my friend Derek spoke at my church on Mother's Day and said these touching important words: "I suppose that in a strict sense, actually giving birth to children is a prerequisite for motherhood. And yet, it seems entirely possible to give birth to a child without ever becoming a mother. If that is true, there must be something more to motherhood than just the act of bringing children into the world." He continued by quoting a church leader who never married or had children, though she deeply wanted to, "Motherhood is more than bearing children, though it is certainly that. It is the essence of who we are as women. It defines our very identity, our divine stature and nature, and the unique traits our Father gave us ... As daughters of our Heavenly Father, and as daughters of Eve, we are all mothers and we have always been mothers. Our calling is to love and help lead the rising generation through the dangerous streets of mortality."

And so I am comforted and reminded that in the end I did become a mother. I serve multiple purposes at this stage in my life; providing that loving mother figure to my step-daughter, allowing myself to grow in unexpected ways. Yet my most challenging act of service is to partner with my dear husband to strengthen each other. Finally I am helping to guide young citizens to live meaningful and productive lives. I have no regrets and feel I am living a rich life that also pleases my Heavenly Father.

Ryan M., 37
Registered Social Worker
Ontario, Canada

I am a gay man who has decided not to have children. I am college educated, work full-time in human services, go to University part time, have a partner, many friends and a loving family. I could have a child through traditional means, with the help of artificial insemination or adoption. But I have no desire to make a child through traditional means. I am gay, after all! I didn't like the idea of artificial insemination. Asking someone to give up a baby after nine months of carrying it is inhumane. And it would break my heart if the "baby mom" decided to keep the child after nine months of waiting.

I am also afraid of whatever emotional or psychological issues might come with an adopted child. If I had a kid, I'd want to be responsible for it from the beginning of life. With adoption, you are getting a child who has already learned cultural lessons and accumulated baggage. So adoption is out.

When I was young, I thought I wanted kids. I wanted the whole package—wife, 2.5 kids, white picket fence and a dog named Spot. When I became comfortable with my sexuality, I thought, "Okay, the wife thing is out but everything else is still doable." After many years I have concluded that my desire for "everything else" came from wanting to fit into a cookie cutter image of what an adult is supposed to be.

I like kids. It would be fun to watch them grow and learn. I have discovered, however, that they are not for me. I am happy with my current life path.

Phoena, 38

Writer

Texas

I suppose I was born without a biological clock. I don't recall ever wanting children yet can't think of any particular incident that drove me to childfreedom.

When I was ten or eleven, I was playing Barbies with a group of friends. All of us said our Barbies were married to our Kens and the couples were going to live happily ever after. Then the three of them had their Barbies excitedly tell their Kens, "Oh, Ken, we're gonna have a baby!" I recall my response: "Ug! *My* Barbie isn't getting pregnant right away!" They all looked puzzled and said, "Well, that's what you DO when you get married." Even at that young age, it just sounded wrong. Surely there had to be more to life than rushing from childhood into motherhood? I didn't know WHAT my Barbie wanted to do with her life, but I knew getting pregnant right away was NOT IT. The fact that my friends felt differently didn't change my opinion; I was always too stubborn to cave to peer pressure.

A few years later when I was in junior high, a friend said, "It's so exciting that we're almost in high school. Pretty soon we'll be graduating and then we'll get married and start having babies!" I remember being absolutely horrified—we were kids ourselves still! Why couldn't we enjoy the rest of our childhood? Why be in such a hurry to be moms? What happened to having goals and dreams?

By high school I learned that I'd never have to have babies because birth control could not only *delay* motherhood but prevent it altogether. What a relief! I'd been afraid my only options in life were wife-and-mother or nun. Thank you, Margaret Sanger! So whenever an adult would say to my teenaged-self, "After you grow up and have kids ..." I would respond with, "I'm not planning on having children. I want to see the world." The adults often replied, "Oh, that's SO CUTE. We ALL said that when we were your age." I knew that wasn't true; my peers weren't saying it!

Now, twenty years later, I'm still perfectly content without children. With regard to parenting, I can't picture any benefits, only drawbacks. All too often I was told I would regret my decision, but instead I feel more confident every year.

Lisa Habig, 38

Army Wife/College Student

Oahu, Hawaii

I am thirty-eight years old and I am an Army wife as well as a full-time college student. My husband is on active duty and we currently reside in Schofield Barracks on the island of Oahu, Hawaii.

When my husband and I were newly married, we thought we were both eager to start a family. After a year of trying, we went to a specialist. I was immediately told that I was "too old" and that I should have come in years ago. Well, I was not married years ago! I remember that even then, I had doubts in my heart about being a parent. My blood work came out fine. At that point, the doctor wanted me to have an HSG—an X-ray that determines whether your tubes are blocked. I began to panic, thinking, "Is this really what I want? Do I want to go through all this trouble simply to have a baby?" On the day of the procedure, I could not go through with it. I ran out of the room. As I was sitting on a bench in the hospital, crying, my husband sat down next to me and asked, "Don't you want to have kids?" I looked him straight in the eye and replied, "No, I really don't." The truth hit me with such finality ... I couldn't believe how good it felt to say it out loud. Then, to my shock and surprise, he said, "I don't want to have kids, either." I'd had NO idea he was feeling the same doubts. We had always prided ourselves on our good communication, so we were surprised that neither of us knew how the other was feeling. My husband has known from a young age that he did not want to be a father, but I think it was easier for him. There is not nearly as much societal pressure on a man to become a parent as there is a woman. I believe that women are capable of far more than bearing and raising children.

Another big part of our decision to stop trying is that we both believe God should be the one to decide who has children and who does not. God has a different plan for our lives and we are okay with that. I have always felt that children should not be created in labs or Petri dishes.

I guess I've known for a long time that I am not "maternal," but the pressure from society and my family was difficult to handle. When you are a woman who doesn't want/have children, there is a negative stigma as well as a firm line drawn between you and the "mommy club." It can be lonely, particularly when all of your friends have children.

My husband and I are happy with our decision. I guess it is in part circumstances and in part our own decision; either way, it is what's best for us. We do not feel as though we are missing out—quite the opposite. We love the freedom we have to come and go as we like. We can spend our money on ourselves or whatever we like and don't have to answer to anyone but ourselves. We have been called "selfish" and that's okay. We know the truth. We have three four-legged and furry "kids"; they are plenty for us!

Cherie J. Collins, 39

Teacher

Orlando, Florida

I chose to be child-free after being raised in an *Eight is enough* household. My mother was a religious fanatic and believed that being a good Catholic meant turning her house into a foster care home. Although she birthed three of us, she felt the need to take in five more children before I was out of diapers. Her decision was nowhere near as selfless as it looked, and it was the main reason I decided not to become a parent.

Naturally, trying to take care of eight kids ranging in age from one to eleven was overwhelming for my mother. After we reached an age when we could monitor each other, she basically let the older ones parent the younger ones as in some strange version of *Lord of the Flies*. She locked us outside and would only let us in if nature's call was a true emergency. Because Miami was hot during the summer, she installed a water fountain that offered the same water that came from the hot hose. She didn't want us to interrupt her soap operas, which she watched while smoking cigarettes, drinking from a bottle of Manischewitz white wine, and waiting for my father to come home from work.

I realized early on that these siblings were not blood-related because they did not have my same last name; still, I did not hesitate to claim them as blood relations and defend them to anyone outside of my family. However, I could not understand why my mother made it a point to remind me, my older sister, and younger brother that we were "not any more special" than the foster children just because we had been in her womb.

Fast forward to my current age of thirty-nine, when most of my friends, family, and co-workers have children and ask incessantly when I am going to marry and have a child of my own. It is these memories of my mother—who willingly took on the role of parent to many but never was much of a mother to me—that remind me not everyone should become a mother. I have never felt my biological clock ticking, even though my sisters ended up becoming mothers after having the same childhood. I do not want to let society pressure me into having kids and then end up resenting my life and using alcohol to escape reality.

People assume that I hate or dislike kids, but this is completely false. My profession is all about children. I am a teacher, which means I can enjoy some aspects of care-giving while still being able to leave my "children" at the end of the day.

Jody LaFlen, 39

College Dean

Bellevue, Washington

My dreams have always been big and varied. When I was very little, I wanted to be a ballerina/Solid Gold Dancer. A few years later, I wanted to own a chain of bakeries. After the Challenger disaster (which happened when I was in eighth grade), I aspired to be an astronaut, concentrating my studies on astronomy and space travel. In high school, I added the U.S. Presidency to my list.

In college I did not feel the same passion for the advanced calculus I needed for a career in space travel, so I studied archaeology. After a few years of fieldwork in the Near East, I went to graduate school in Higher Education Administration. I am the youngest Dean ever at the college where I now work. One dream I never had was a life with children. From an early age, well-meaning adults would ask, "How will you manage to be a Solid Gold Dancer/President once you have kids?" My answer was always the same—that kids were not in my life plan. The response I received was invariably, "Oh, you'll change your mind once you meet the right man."

I have traveled the world and speak multiple languages. I have jumped out of planes, run marathons, flown a helicopter and an airplane, hang-glided, lindy-hopped, produced fashion shows, hosted countless charity fundraisers, rescued animals, climbed mountains and been certified in scuba. None of these achievements would have been possible if I had had kids. I am very fortunate to have found a soul mate, a husband who shares my bucket list (minus the shark dive), and my desire not to procreate. We enjoy being an aunt and uncle but do not feel the need to add to the world population.

Some people accuse me of being selfish, opting to achieve my dreams rather than sacrificing them to have children I do not want. Perhaps they are right. I work ten to twelve hour days to help make a college education accessible to all who want one. Thousands of students have received degrees because of my work. I will turn forty next year. I am often told that I will wake up one morning and feel the need to have kids, but I know now, as I have known all along—that my dreams do not include having offspring.

Wendy, 39
International Education Consultant
Northern Virginia, USA

My husband and I have enjoyed fourteen and a half years of marriage so far. When we married, we assumed we would have a life much like everyone else's: enjoying our marriage for a few years, working, and finally—after spending two years as U.S. Peace Corps Volunteers—starting a family. In fact, during our engagement and early years of marriage, my husband kept saying that one reason he married me was that he knew I would make a great mother for our children—and I wanted to be that for and with him.

After a few years trying, I was finally diagnosed with Premature Ovarian Failure (aka Primary Ovarian Insufficiency), resulting in infertility. With only eight percent chance of getting pregnant naturally, our only choices were egg donation or adoption. After years of soul searching, we finally accepted being a family of two, as fate had determined. I define myself as "childfree-by-circumstance." I am not "childfree by choice," as not having children was never my "choice." However, I am not "childless." That implies we are missing something, that we are lacking, incomplete. Life is full of surprises, curveballs, and unexpected lessons and opportunities. The only thing we "chose" to do was go with the flow life has given us, and find purpose, meaning, and fun in other ways.

With a professional background in child development and education, and also an interest in and experiences with living/working overseas, I saw my infertility as a doorway into pursuing my passion—helping children in developing countries to improve their quality of life and have better educational opportunities. I can travel for months at a time and help thousands of children and their parents, as opposed to the few who might live under my roof if we had adopted. My husband is supportive, and recently has been encouraging me to look for fulltime work overseas. How many people can say they have been in five countries in four years, focusing entirely on improving the quality of education?

Infertility can be a curse, but only if you let it be. For me, infertility has made me stronger and more adventurous. Do I feel pangs of sadness and regret? Of course, I am human. But infertility can also give you a sense of freedom and allow you to commit to causes outside of yourself and immediate family that parents do not often have the time or energy to promote. I can't imagine my life any other way.

Ramona Creel, 39
Photographer / RVer

Naples, Florida

As we travel the country as full-time RVers, folks often ask Matt and me if we have children. When I respond that we are "child-free," most people have no clue what that means. I explain that we don't want to have children—an entirely foreign concept to the majority of Americans. Some are fascinated by the possibilities of life without kids, but others can't even begin to understand why we would make such a bizarre life choice. I like to tell people that I had a maternal instinct once—when I was about twelve—but then it went away and has never bothered me since. Perhaps it's genetic. My friends couldn't wait to be old enough to babysit, but I didn't want to look after other people's kids. Even the good ones were too much work—keeping them entertained and out of trouble until their parents came home. Oh sure, I played with dolls, but I always preferred the adventures of my adult Barbies to babies that cried and peed and spit up. Barbie's pink glamour camper made a lasting impression on my young mind—that must be why I chose to travel instead of procreate!

It's not that I dislike children as a species. I'm quite fond of the "good" ones—laughing toddlers and sharp-witted adolescents and teens with strong, independent personalities. But I have very little tolerance for kids who are allowed by their parents to act like brats, and never once did I feel the urge to take one home with me. I'm completely content to play with them, get them wound up, and give them back to their parents. I compare a child to a Picasso hanging in a museum—I don't have to own it to enjoy it!

Fortunately I married a man who has always agreed with me—ever since we started dating at the tender age of sixteen. Early in our marriage, Matt got a little sentimental around the holidays, romanticizing the idea of Christmas mornings with children—until we spent a Noël with a friend and her six-year-old. That cured him pretty quick! Ever since we hit the road as full-time RVers, we've been having too much fun to even consider cluttering things up with kids. We go where we want, when we want, without worrying about school vacations and truancy officers. We can eat strange, exotic food instead of chicken fingers. We live simply, in less than 200 square feet, entirely sans kindercrap. We can focus on our own projects instead of spending our time attending PTA meetings. We've traded diapers and preschools and college funds for freedom, leisure time, and personal fulfillment. I can't imagine having to park in one place for the next eighteen years, putting my dreams and goals off until the nest was emptied, missing out on the amazing experiences we have regularly while traveling the country.

I'm also using my freedom to work on a series of travel and photography books (www.RamonaCreel.com). Call it selfish if you want. We call it "living the life."

Jennifer Waber Artale, 39
Publishing
Brooklyn, New York

I am thirty-nine years old, happily married and childless. My negative feelings about children have been strong for many years. I grew up an only child. An only child is a lonely child, but I digress. When I was ten, an amazing thing happened. My mother became pregnant. Finally, my lonely days were over. Maybe the child would be way younger than me, but at least I would finally have a sibling.

Well, my brother was born and that was it. We brought him home and it all started. The crying, the snot, the drool, the stinky diapers .... I hated him. Or, at least, as I learned over time, I hated kids. During my first and only diaper change, my brother peed on me. I loathed it all. I knew I could never handle it. I was the obvious babysitting solution for my parents, but I just couldn't do it. I hated hearing him cry and scream and I hated it when he stank. Why would I ever choose to be around that?

I have seen what it's like to raise a child. I have been a part of it. For all the hated moments, there were some great ones. I feel I am fortunate to know what it is like to have a child, but I've never been solely responsible for one. For that, I wholeheartedly thank my parents.

As I get older and realize this is my last shot at experiencing the wonders of childbirth, I wonder whether I'm doing the right thing. What about depriving my parents of the pleasure of being grandparents? That weighs on me heavily. All I need to do is remind myself of the torturous, daily routines that must take place in order to raise a child, and then I don't worry about it anymore.

Forties

Lisa, 40
Creative Business Owner
Manhattan, New York

I knew I did not want to have children when I was still a child. Maybe it was that I was always a driven dreamer, or perhaps in another life I was a mother of five or more and felt this round I would sit motherhood out. However, growing up, I had an innate desire to create. I would spend hours in my room writing a play or making a painting or building an outdoor model horse ranch from rocks and twigs. I found that my creations were always so fulfilling in and of themselves that they "replaced" any biological desire to procreate.

When I was a teenager, though I loved boys and socializing, I was petrified of getting pregnant. I remained a virgin until I was twenty out of fear I would end up like those girls in the frightening teen pregnancy commercials, trapped forever. Everything about the 9-5, picket fence, typical family lifestyle, terrified me. I saw the "average Joe" lifestyle as a negation of who I was, and I knew I was not built for it. I have always been a free spirit who loves to learn, discover, and explore. Raising my baby sister who came along when I was ten years old taught me that family life was the opposite of freedom.

Throughout my twenties I enjoyed singlehood while my need for artistic expression continued to grow stronger, as did my opinions about exactly how I wanted to live my life. That vision consciously never involved having/raising children, even when I met the man of my dreams in my late twenties. We eventually married and are child free by choice now, twelve years later.

In my twenties I happily focused on my full-time career as a creative business owner. The way I nurture my business and creative projects is quite similar to how a mother nurtures her child. For me, the only difference is the form of the creation.

I've always had a vision for my life and have taken great strides in getting to where I want to be, with absolutely no regrets. There is too much in this world to see and discover to be stuck at home all day doing laundry, cleaning dishes, and helping with homework. I prefer to donate my time to helping clean up the damage done to the environment by overpopulation.

Michele Gillis, 41

Management

Pembroke Pines, Florida

I'm living in Pembroke Pines, Florida with seven dogs. Besides animals, I love music and art, traveling and shopping.

I was the oldest in a home of two girls, four years apart in age. I was about four years old when I began to wish I was an only child. I relished being alone with my parents and preferred the company of adults. I remember being annoyed with childish behavior even though I was a child myself. My parents forced my baby sister down my throat. I always had to play with her and allow her to tag along with my friends. I knew even then I would never want children of my own.

Not only did dolls not interest me, but thoughts of being a mommy never entered my mind. Through the teenage years, girlfriends would daydream about getting pregnant and having babies, as if that would be like winning the lotto. I recall an incident when I was about twelve years old. My closest girlfriend at the time was bragging about having started her period. She was enamored with the fact that she could actually get pregnant and have a baby. I thought she was completely insane.

My initial reason for not wanting children was more fear than anything else. When I would think of babies, the first thing that came to mind was that babies scream, cry and spit up (not in order of importance). The puking part bothered me most. For me, the sight, smell or sound of vomit would send me into a major panic attack, to the point that I would have crashed through a plate glass window to get away. I would shake, sweat profusely and my heart would race and pound out of my chest as if I was having a heart attack. Have a kid? No way. Kids throw up, and they throw up frequently. They are always sick and responsible for getting their parents sick. As ridiculous as it sounds, that was my number one reason for not wanting children. Number two reason: pregnancy. Pregnancy equals morning sickness, which equals vomit. I never shared my vomit affliction with anyone for fear I would be labeled a lunatic.

It wasn't until I was an adult in my thirties that I found out I wasn't as mentally unstable as I thought. While surfing the Internet I stumbled across an article about Denise Richards, the actress once married to Charlie Sheen, who openly admitted she had a severe aversion to vomit. There is a name for it: emetophobia. Emetophobics are afraid of vomit. Not just of being sick themselves, but others vomiting. Just the mention of the word "vomit" can send an emetophobe into hysterics.

Apparently most emetophobics avoid children at all costs; they fear morning sickness, are afraid of having to care for a sick child or having the child make them sick. The childfree and the emetophobe would be a match made in heaven.

I can think of nothing about having children that is rewarding or fulfilling. I can't explain this; so many other people see them as "miracles" or "blessings from God." Clearly I am the exception and not the rule.

The mere thought of being pregnant mortifies me. It is beyond my comprehension why anyone would do such a horrible thing to their bodies or themselves. Envisioning myself pregnant fills me with sheer and utter horror. Getting fat and never being able to lose the weight. The irreversible damage a pregnancy inflicts on a body—the stretch marks, sagging stomach and drooping boobs, not to mention the unmentionable "body part." No thank you. Would it change sex? I wasn't about to compromise my sex life. I heard story after story as well as complaints from numerous men about how a woman's sex life changed for the worse, how she lost her sex drive, how sex didn't feel the same to either her or her husband because squeezing a baby out left you stretched out.

Changing dirty diapers, being thrown up on, getting woken up in the middle of the night by a crying baby, giving up my social life, having to spend money on a child, having to put up with a dirty house and having to childproof it ... on and on. None of this was anything I was willing to put up with.

I want to live life to the fullest. I can't think of one positive thing to be gained from having a child, not one, not even love. I know many more folks who hate their parents, never see them or are estranged than those who love their parents with that "unconditional" love that only naïve people believe in. That's another risk I was not willing to take.

Was I willing to make all those sacrifices, damage my body, spend my life savings, turn myself into a neurotic, nervous wreck, only to have my child tell me to go "fuck" myself when they turned sixteen? Watch them become a hardened criminal, prostitute or drug addict? Or what if after high school my child moved away and for the next thirty years the only time I ever heard from them was a phone call at Christmas or a card on Mother's Day if I was lucky? What if my child grew up blaming me for everything wrong in their life? I just didn't see the point.

My husband and I have been married for five years. I considered having a baby with him—for a split second—when we first married. We firmly decided not to bring a child into the world; we were enjoying our lives too much and it wasn't financially feasible. Two years ago, divine intervention made my decision final. I was diagnosed with cervical cancer and lost all my plumbing.

I have never regretted my decision to remain childfree.

Yana Sorokina, 42

Psychologist

Ufa, Bashkortostan, Russia

I am a psychologist with an advanced degree in mathematics and programming. I'm not married and live in a big city.

The main reason I don't want children is that I don't wish to bring new sufferers into this world; life is too hard. Also, I do not have the financial means; a child has the right to a separate room, which I cannot afford. I don't want to bring a child up in poverty and I don't want to make my own living conditions worse. Also, I am against giving birth without a husband.

About myself: I am a vegan for ethical reasons. I live in a one-room apartment with two cats who used to be strays. I am happy. I enjoy my solitude. Work makes me tired, and I like to come home and spend time alone with my cats. I have a beloved; he sometimes comes to visit. But I live alone.

This world is precarious; health, money, and a husband can all be lost in a moment. No matter how secure a life seems, there is always danger of a global cataclysm, natural disasters—flooding, earthquakes, and meteorites falling. Then all the money will turn to worthless pieces of paper. To bring someone into this cruel world without any guarantees of safety is selfish.

The Earth is already overpopulated, but people continue to produce new copies of themselves for the sake of their own egos. Today, world population reaches seven billion. One billion would be enough for prosperity.

Dedra Kaye DeHart, 43
Machine Operator
Clay City, Illinois

I don't recall ever making a conscious decision not to have children; I just naturally did not desire them. When I was dating my ex-husband he asked, "How many kids do you want?" I gulped and replied, "As few as possible, like, uh, none ..." He seemed relieved that I didn't want any, yet at the same time he would make comments like, "One of these days I'll switch your birth control pills for placebos so you'll get pregnant." Thankfully, we were not married long and I was never subjected to a forced pregnancy just to produce an heir for the old family team. When some older ladies learned that we didn't plan on having any kids they would say, "Why did you bother getting married?" Well, it wasn't to have children. It might have been a short-lived marriage, but at least I didn't make the mistake many people do and have a baby to try to keep things going when they obviously were at a dead stop.

Anonymous, 43
Health Information Management Supervisor
Colorado

When I was in high school in the '80s, the problem of teenage pregnancy was starting to get public attention. What was once a forbidden topic was now openly discussed. My authority figures at the time, parents and teachers, were telling us teenage girls that if we got pregnant, it would "ruin our lives." That any time we had to spend with our friends would be over. That the chances of us getting an education would be slim. Opportunities that were once open to us would become unavailable. That caring for a child would make us unable to live a free and happy life. I listened, and over the course of my life have carried that line of thinking into adulthood. I've often asked myself, "Okay, *now* am I ready for life as I know it to come to an end? *Now* am I ready for my friendships to be over ? *Now* am I ready for opportunities such as learning a new language or traveling to be out of reach?" What I've found is that no matter what stage of life I've been in, the answer to those questions has always been "No." My decision to be child-free is a decision to keep my life as is, with the future still wide open, even at forty-three years of age.

Cynthia Southern, 43

Claims Analyst

Denver, Colorado

I chose not to have children at age twelve. Although I didn't want to raise children, I always wanted to get married and have a wonderful husband. I also wanted to have a career, travel, write and do the things I love. Education was important to me. I earned a BA in History and have a full-time career.

I love having the freedom to do whatever my heart desires. I have a career, a wonderful husband who also does not want children and a myriad of hobbies and activities I enjoy. I also believe that too many people exist on earth; there is already so much starvation and poverty. It is a responsible environmental choice not to have children.

With no children to worry about or care for, I can give my husband the time he deserves. We can go to dinner without having to hire a babysitter. I can sleep in on Saturdays and holidays. We can watch movies and choose activities that aren't "family friendly." We avoid "family friendly" venues and activities because there is no fun, peace or quiet when children and rude parents in attendance. "Family friendly" translates to "boring."

Nothing ruins a romantic dinner like a screaming baby. We spend a lot of time at home where we are assured disruptive children won't be around. We have two restaurants we enjoy and give them our business because they do not encourage children to eat there. Recently my husband and I created a website dedicated to the issue of loud children in public places called www.NoChildrenPlease.com.

Peer pressure forces many people to have children when they would rather not. For me children would be a burden and a prison sentence. Being child-free is not an affliction. It is liberation.

I love life with my husband. I have published magazine articles and am planning on writing a work of popular history. I will be traveling to Europe to research my book. If I had children I would have neither the time nor the finances to devote to such pursuits.

Dr. Ilyssa Hershey, 43

Psychologist

New York

I don't remember having or wanting dolls. I don't remember playing house and pretending I was a mommy with a baby. The only toy I remember like that was "Baby Alive." I loved that she could eat and poop! I don't know if I asked for it because of a commercial or if my mom just bought it for me. I had many friends and lived in a suburban neighborhood in a good school district. We rode our bikes after school and watched cartoons. I was by no means a tomboy … not even close. I was very girly—into pretty clothes, hair, makeup, etc. Danskin and tights were "in" back then and I wore them with matching tights and hair barrettes.

When I was around ten my parents began to yell and fight often. My father became aggressive with my mother and the police were called on a few occasions. My brother and I witnessed some of this violence, and I remember not only being terrified but also embarrassed that the neighbors heard and saw it.

My parents finally divorced and my brother, mother and I moved to another neighborhood. My mother was not able to afford to continue living there and my father was not helping in any way. I didn't know the term "dead-beat" dad … but that's what he was. I was in the eighth grade. It was a difficult transition to leave your friends, school and childhood home. Probably more traumatic than I cared to admit at the time. Realizing that I felt rejected by my father and uprooted from all that I found safe, my mom decided I should go to therapy. Smart lady! My therapy continued until I turned thirty. But I don't want to get ahead of myself.

My mom got a job and started to go to school at night to finish her college degree. She was strong and took care of us. I was in awe of her ability to move forward. She was and continues to be a great source of support and love.

I finished high school, entered college, and graduated with a BA in Psychology. I had known all through middle and high school that I wanted to be a Psychologist. I was that friend that everyone went to for advice, support and acceptance. So I entered a five year doctoral program. While I was going to school full-time and focusing on that goal of being called "Doctor," my friends were getting married and having babies. I wanted a boyfriend but never longed for a baby or a family. I was jealous of the marriages, not the kids.

My therapy focused on my low self-esteem and inability to express anger or any other negative emotions. My father thought women should be seen and not heard. I only felt good about myself when others reflected that for me. I didn't finish therapy until a few months before I got married. The subject of having a baby or being a mother never came up. It was not in my conscious or unconscious mind. I simply wasn't interested.

I married for the wrong reasons. All my friends were married and going on kid number two or three and I just wanted to be married. I had recently received my doctorate in Psychology and was working in my first job in that capacity. During this marriage I developed TMJ and depression. I was able to see patterns and red flags for other people, but not for myself. The need to have a partner and not be alone was just too great. I was also no longer in therapy. The only saving grace was that he didn't care about kids one way or another. Thank god!

Within our first year of marriage my husband's brother committed suicide. He was only forty-two and they were very close. A year later his other brother died of a massive heart attack. My husband became very depressed and thought we needed to make more family members. He thought we should have a child. I was so distraught for him I didn't think too much about it and we started trying. It didn't happen. So I went to a fertility specialist. They went through all the common intrusive tests and came up with a diagnosis of "Undiagnosed Infertility." They said all my parts were working fine. I realized this news didn't upset me. The doctor urged me to take fertility medication. That was the first time a tiny voice inside myself was able to push through enough to be heard. I said no to the next level of treatment. I went home.

Then came the years that included all these family parties and holidays where I was asked at least once each event, "When are you going to have kids?" All my cousins were having kids … we were the only ones who were not. Do you know how hard it is to be polite and loving while you say you don't want kids? Yeah, I said it, but I got *that* look and *those* questions. We stopped going to family functions.

One day my period was almost two weeks late. We weren't using birth control but we were not trying either. Most women would be so thrilled and excited. Not me. This was the second time the little tiny voice inside me was able to push through. And then my "Ah Ha" Moment. I was in the bathroom sitting on the toilet peeing. I went to wipe myself and looked at the white toilet paper, which I did every time for those two weeks. It was covered in blood. My heart opened and my lungs were able to take in the deepest breaths they had taken in years. Tears were running down my cheeks. I have never been so happy in my life! "Hello, Ilyssa, where have you been? I have been trying to talk to you and lead you to *you*. You have not noticed *you* for years."

This was the moment that I became AWARE of me. I didn't want children. There I said it. I DON'T WANT TO HAVE A BABY!! The dam broke and the waters came rushing in. I had spent so much time trying to do the right thing and please everyone around me, the theme of my life and my therapy. I sacrificed ME. This was a moment I will never forget, the release, the relief.

I started attending family functions again. It was so different. I felt so good about myself and others felt it, too. Once I became absolutely sure of my choices and who I am and what I wanted, I began not to mind or care about the opinions and comments and questions of others. They just didn't upset me anymore. I no longer had to defend myself because I no longer had to convince MYSELF that I was making the right choice. Those around me began to feel and see my power and glow, and the questions and comments soon stopped.

The divorce came a few years later. It took a bit longer to hear the tiny voice regarding my marriage.

Then I met Eric. We have a loving life together—wonderful careers and a beautiful home. We are both childfree by choice. We both feel complete and at peace.

I don't need motherhood to define me. Life is good, I am good. I am.

Theresa Merrick Calhill, 44

Office Administrator

Burlington, Ontario

I didn't choose not to be a parent, much like I didn't choose to fall in love with my husband twenty years ago. It just happened. I couldn't control it and I didn't plan it.

I don't feel as though I had a choice. I'm just wired differently. I don't have a maternal instinct at all. Sure, I have five cats I look after, love and adore, but that's different and people who compare pet parenthood to human parenthood need to grow up.

Nothing will change my mind. No amount of cajoling or speeches from parents or government incentives will make me want children.

I had a wonderful childhood. My parents (my mother in particular) sacrificed a lot to raise me and my brother. Our house was the one where all the kids would hang out. All our friends thought we had the "coolest parents ever." My parents loved and provided for us and gave us everything they had in order to make our lives as comfortable and happy as possible and I'm a better person because of it. However, I don't "owe" my parents anything and I certainly don't owe them grandchildren, which, believe it or not, some have argued.

I had my tubes tied over ten years ago. No questions asked, and no regrets. Luckily for me, I had a very understanding doctor who did not make me jump through hoops, or interview my husband or question my ability to decide what I wanted to do with my own body and soul.

I no more want to be a mother than I want to be an accountant but when I declare the former I am STILL met with sneers and nasty comments and questions.

So, if anyone asks me why I don't want to be a parent, I just say that I don't have a choice. I was born this way. Much as some women have a burning desire to be a mother, I do not. It's that simple.

Linda Sear, 44
Administrative Professional
Edmonton, AB Canada

I started to babysit as a teenager, first for a neighbor, and later at the age of twenty for a couple. I remember feeling I was not 'cut out' to be a parent; I just didn't have the patience or natural maternal feelings.

For six more years my feelings grew in intensity until at the age of twenty-six, I finally went to my female physician and asked to have my tubes tied. This was back in the early 1990s. I lived in a small town in Manitoba—a procreation happy and family-oriented community—where this procedure was unheard of. I finally found a male doctor in another town half an hour away who agreed to do it. He asked over and over if I was sure, because reversing the procedure would be quite costly, in the thousands of dollars. I was sure. I had the tubal ligation done (laser method), and I have never ever looked back or regretted my decision.

I am adopted. My late father was verbally abusive; otherwise we didn't have a lot to do with each other. I was either yelled at for doing something bad or ignored. My mother doted more on me—I am the youngest—but she was, and still is, smothering and oppressive. My parents were older, already in their fifties, by the time I was in high school, so I couldn't talk to them about anything. They were not 'hip,' modern people, and their way of thinking was old school. While they were always very good financial providers, and I never lacked for anything, our relationship was not satisfying or positive. (I am grateful that they sent me to attend an expensive private Christian high school from grades 10-12—it was a big improvement over junior high.) I had an older sister who was bossy, sometimes mean to me, and had a terrible temper when angry. She will not sit down and calmly discuss issues. Instead she keeps all her hostility and rage inside; then it flares up if you *do* try to talk to her. Our relationship has never been close, but now we have no contact. Interestingly, my mom and *her* older sister also do not have a close relationship—despite living in the same small town—and have fought on many occasions about family matters. They are also no longer in contact. Their relationship with their own mother was difficult. As for my father, I learned from my late aunt before she died that his father was very hard on him, just like he was on me. I have always worried that if I had children, I would repeat my parents' mistakes.

I always longed for parents like the ones on the television show, *Family Ties*. Mrs. Keaton was open-minded, a positive thinker, and not easily flustered; her children could talk to her about anything. My mother was exactly the opposite.

When I was about six, my mother told me I was adopted. This did not help my self-esteem. My birth mother had me at age nineteen, her second 'oops!' As a teenager I already felt unloved by my father and controlled and smothered by my domineering mother; it didn't help my self-esteem that my real mother had given me up. When I was twenty I tried to find her or my birth father, but even though my efforts were unsuccessful, that search finally gave me some closure. (I did finally locate a half sister who was born two years before me.) I had already decided that I did not want a kid born out of wedlock and feeling like 'a mistake.' I was lucky to avoid pregnancy at a young age, because I was less than diligent about birth control once I was sexually active—my feeble attempts to find love. I believe I was never fertile anyway.

I also observed my close friends who had kids (planned or not) and how it changed their lives and affected my friendship with them; I resented that I could no longer spend quality alone-time with them, or visit them without a screaming baby howling for their attention. They were truly "tied down," and I did not want that for myself. I relish my freedom and independence to this day. I need to come and go as I please and spend money on whatever I want without some kid strapped to my legs. My life has had plenty of hardships, including my current financial situation, and I simply cannot afford to provide for kids in any case.

I believe in pro-choice, and if I *had* become pregnant, I would have had an abortion. I see many younger, unmarried girls these days who take up many seats on the transit bus with their huge SUV size strollers and I look at them in pity. I may not be the poster girl for adoption, but I don't understand how they can selfishly keep their children when they are clearly not mature or responsible enough. They are no more mother-material than

I am. I think they kept their children out of guilt or in order to ride the welfare system.

Anonymous, 45
Homemaker
Frankfort, Kentucky

I decided not to procreate when I was a child. When I was given a doll for Christmas, I just wasn't interested and put it down on the floor. I wanted a train set like the one my brothers received. As a teenager, I was still never interested in babies; I saw how difficult it was to be a mother.

My mom had eight of us and I am the only one who didn't want kids. Everyone always told me, "You will change your mind." I knew I never would, but they didn't realize how strongly I felt about the issue. So I was on birth control for a long time, starting at nineteen. Finally at age thirty I got sterilized. I was thinking, "Why not get sterilized? Then it will be my final decision; I'll never have to worry about birth control again."

My family doesn't know how I feel; they're just not me. I have no maternal instinct and no interest in kids. I just couldn't handle the noise they make and the messes. There would be no time for me. The expense is simply not worth it. Kids take a lot of time. I see how tough it is for people, especially single mothers. It would be a nightmare for me. I am glad to this day that I made the choice to be childfree. There are also too many people in the world already and the pollution and poverty are getting worse. I am proud to be childfree by choice.

T.A., 45
Business Manager
Bothell, Washington

I always thought I would have kids. I am unlike a lot of other people in this book who knew early on that it was not something they would ever do.

As I grew up I thought I would sense that the time had come to get pregnant and do the family thing. However, I've always been mystified by my friends who were so in love with babies or little kids. I did not "get" the attraction, but I still thought having kids would be a part of my life at some point. Isn't that what we women are "supposed" to do? It's programmed into us to believe our lives will be incomplete without them.

So I finished college, started a job, and then went back to grad school. I put off the decision on children until later …. until it was basically forced on me. My husband and I found ourselves unexpectedly pregnant. I was thirty-four. We had used birth control, but the method had failed.

Getting pregnant was the last thing on my mind at that time. I was immediately forced to make a very, very difficult decision. When we looked at the results of the over the counter pregnancy test, both my husband and I responded with a "Oh, no …"

It was not the time or the place or the plan. So less than three weeks into the journey I swallowed some pills that ended what could have been a child.

We realized that our lives would have to change drastically if we were to have kids. Neither of us wanted that. Our finances were not in order, and I wouldn't be able to get the paid time off necessary to go through a pregnancy. It was just too much and frankly part of me was terrified of going through the physical act of being pregnant and bearing children then dealing with all the issues, baggage, problems, of raising a child. My husband is also eleven years older, and although he agreed that if I wanted children he would go along with it, he wasn't enthusiastic. The whole parent thing did not feel right for us.

I think for me the core issue of why I chose to do what I did (with consensus from my husband) is that to me taking on the responsibility of being a parent is HUGE. To me it was a job that seemed overwhelming in nature, and it would be something that must be taken very seriously because you are responsible for another human being in every way. For some reason there was part of me that was incapable of making that kind of commitment, and actually feared that commitment. And there was part of me that did not want to be burdened with that commitment. I felt like I already had enough on the table.

I think too many people go in to being a parent without any thought of the responsibility involved, and that seems inexcusable to me. It is the most important job on the planet, and far too people don't give it the purpose or value necessary.

Because I take that kind of commitment very seriously I simply was too overwhelmed and afraid to take it on.

It's important that women realize being childless does not mean you are less of a woman, or that somehow you don't measure up—that there is something "wrong" with you. I can't count the number of friends who told me that if they could do it all again they would not have children.

What is interesting about my story is that eleven years later, at the age of forty-five, I have in some ways regretted not going through with that pregnancy. Sometimes I wonder what our child would have been like, and every year when that time of year comes around, I think about it.

As I have gotten older I realize the gifts we can still offer the world without having to bear our own children. I enjoy spending time with my niece and nephew and volunteering at a local middle school. Ironically my husband has a son from a previous marriage who really has not been part of our lives until the last two years. He has three kids. So imagine going from having none of your own to being a step-grandmother at forty-five.

In a way my story comes full circle.

Glenna Neilson, 46

Retired

Olympia, Washington

For me, there was never any question of wanting to be a mother. From early on (as early as age six or so), whenever I would hear things like "When you grow up and have kids of your own ..." and later when friends and siblings would spout, "When I have kids ..." what immediately came to mind was "I'M NOT GOING TO!" But, very much like people who know early on they are homosexual, I didn't dare express my feelings on the subject. I instinctively knew I was going against the grain in a way I was not yet prepared to defend. Even as an adult, I've often chosen to stay quiet in an effort not to offend others and generally keep the peace.

Hence, in our culture, living with knowing you do not want children is a lot like being a "closeted" homosexual! And yes, like homosexuals, I'd sure appreciate some open-mindedness about the label "child-FREE" (as opposed to "child-LESS"). As I myself have tried not to judge those who crave babies, I'd like to at least see a genuine attempt at NOT judging me for literally being born this way. After all, expecting someone who does NOT want to create children to do it anyway, just because it's "what everyone does" or because "You'll never know what it's like or how special it is until you have one," is just like expecting someone who's same-sex oriented to suddenly be drawn to the opposite sex. It's insensitive, unfair, and downright offensive.

Early on my reasoning was strictly personal. I knew I didn't want to be a mother, I hated the concept of pregnancy, and I didn't like babies. I preferred being with older kids and adults. Later I realized I didn't want to schedule every aspect of my life around children; I wanted the freedom that being child-free allows.

In high school/early college, I started to consider the "global" aspects of having children—such as overpopulation, waste and pollution, depletion of natural resources. My reasoning was no longer limited to how becoming a parent would impact my life on a personal level. I couldn't stand the idea of bringing another person into the world under such conditions and having to explain to them WHY. So, I swore that if I ever felt that urge to be a mother, I would adopt a child instead of creating one.

That's not to say that I haven't enjoyed and valued my life and the world around me; I absolutely have, and continue to. I just happen to be aware that there are now over SEVEN BILLION of us here. All of us want to survive, yet fewer and fewer of us will. The vast majority of those who do survive will not have nearly as good a time as our current generation—even here in the U.S. Worldwide, survival will become more and more challenging as time goes by and the population continues to expand exponentially and resources to deplete. I feel very lucky to be living my life when I am, where I am. Extremely lucky.

Many people assume that those who choose not to have children had a bad childhood, but that is not the case with myself or my husband. In fact, both of us had happy childhoods. Our parents did their best and gave us love and protection, security, etc. While I am the anomaly in my family for not wanting children, my husband and his only sibling both chose not to have them. A big difference between our families is that his parents are supportive and understanding; they actually *agree* with our reasoning. My family, however, judges me for not doing what they did, and actually *pity* me for "missing out" on something they think is so special. They aren't interested in our reasons because they prefer to think of us as "selfish," when in fact it's very much the opposite.

Over the years I have let go of almost every female friend in my life, as they one-by-one became mothers …. I know the desire to move on was mutual; they didn't value my friendship in the same way during or after their transformation, either. They were in a new phase of their lives, and very clearly belonged with other mommies or "wanna-be-mommies." (As for my relations, it's been an exercise in tolerance.) VERY few have remained the same people they were *before* undergoing this transformation into motherhood; these women somehow retained their ability to think about things other than babies/children AND their sense of humor! They're the ones I have kept in my life; there's no disrespect or judgment, and we are honest with each other. Many men change in similar ways, but they are not usually as nauseating or annoying … and they tend to go back to being their old selves eventually, unlike most women.

I am happy to have found a spouse who shares my views. We married when I was thirty-two and he was forty. When he was young he had married a woman who didn't want children, but then changed her mind in her mid-thirties. Their marriage ended for many reasons, but her sudden change of heart was a major one. Obviously the lack of desire to be parents cannot be a couple's only common ground; we have many common interests and beliefs, have no problem finding LOTS of things to do and share besides taking care of (and worrying about) children.

Because we didn't have to consider children, my husband and I were free to relocate to a place we really wanted to live. I was able to quit my job several years ago for "quality of life" reasons, which also enabled us to work hard (outside of my husband's "real" job) toward a future in which he was able to retire early, at fifty-three. This is something most people with kids can't afford financially, but even if they could, they wouldn't have the time, energy or creativity. So now we have a lot of time to enjoy together.

We aren't as into traveling as many CF people (or as people in general think we should be), because we love spending time with our pets and in the home that we worked hard to create. We go places that intrigue us when we want to—usually off season. Not having children to schedule around, we have the flexibility to avoid crowds, and hoards of children when school is out. We prefer to stay local and enjoy what's nearby, and we love that we don't have to cart kids all over the place for this or that event—

all of which results in having a comparatively "smaller footprint."

Because we enjoy the region in which we live, we are able to take our travel trailer to beautiful places on a whim (no, we don't feel guilty, because of everything listed above), and we enjoy sailing—which can be hellish with children. We love walking our dogs together; most couples with kids have to take turns. We take on home projects of all kinds, some of which would be impossible or dangerous with kids underfoot. We enjoy gardening/landscaping, and we love that we have no jungle-gyms or toys and scooters strewn around. We love not having "kid food" in the house, or plastic plates and cups falling out of our cabinets. We enjoy dinners out and live performances, art shows, wine—things that are generally off-limits to kids. We love socializing with our few good friends without needing to accommodate children. We love watching intelligent and sometimes edgy (or *boring* by some people's standards) documentaries and movies without having to wait 'til the kids are asleep. We love sleeping late whenever we feel like it, and having cake for breakfast if we want to.

We have the time to properly research things and make informed decisions. (If only this protected us from making mistakes.) We can donate money that would no doubt be spent on the trivial and temporary wants of the children, and we are planning to leave what would otherwise be their inheritance to charity. We value being available to help friends and neighbors. And, although it can be very frustrating, we're glad to be available to get involved with our small neighborhood community and help out as much as we can.

Not a day goes by that we are not thankful we didn't become parents. I have heard it all over the years—about being lonely in old age, etc. There are no guarantees. I have known many people whose children rarely call or visit, and I've known many whose children make their lives miserable, bringing them nothing but stress and mayhem. My husband and I both feel that we have much more to look forward to together without that unknown variable. We hope to enjoy our self-made freedom and our lives together into our old-age. We realize that we do miss out on certain things, but we also know what those who clutter their lives with children are missing. We have no regrets whatsoever.

Suzanne Mueller, 48

Compliance Manager, Development, and Cellist

Long Island, New York

There are two primary reasons for my being childless by choice:

First, I am a dual-career cellist. I have a demanding, responsible, and substantive "day job," and I am also a professional cellist and manager, booking agent, webmaster, graphic designer, etc., for my ensemble. My partner is a career musician—a freelancer—with erratic hours and a largely unpredictable schedule. Having a child would end the musical part of my life.

Second, I was born with a congenital mobility impairment. Although I always felt loved and valued, I saw what having to cope with that cost my mom and, again, I don't want a child badly enough to risk a similar situation.

My sister is a great mother (as was and is our mom). Being a mother is very important to her and she doesn't mind devoting herself to her son and shaping her world around his needs. I'm frankly more selfish (or self-centered). My independence means too much for me, and I don't have that burning need for motherhood. I don't dislike children—I'm happy to be an aunt—but I have no maternal urges. I've known this since I was about twenty. I wanted to have a tubal ligation then, but the doctors wouldn't believe I could be sure, or that I'd be happy to adopt if I ever really felt the need to be a parent. Both my ex-husband and my partner knew up-front that, if they wanted to be fathers, I was not the woman for them.

Hillari Hunter, 49

Baptist Church Secretary

Chicago, Illinois

The incident that stands out most in my mind happened the summer I was twelve. Ma had begun to lecture both my younger sister and me about the importance of not getting caught with a baby. She made it clear that she was not going to tolerate any out-of-wedlock pregnancies under her roof. Our options would be a) get an abortion or b) get out of her house and take the baby with us. "If any girl goes out there and does what a grown woman does, then she's going to be treated like a grown woman and be expected to handle her own problems," Ma stated. My mother had observed the rise of pregnancies among the girls in the area and the girls my sister and I attended school with. She had no intention of being one of the many mothers going around wringing their hands and sporting extra gray hair because of mistakes made by their daughters. Ma was having a hard enough time just being a divorcee with three kids and no support from my dad.

My oldest first cousin, eighteen at the time, had become an unwed mom a few months earlier. She and her mother, my aunt, had a falling out over it. Feeling slighted by my aunt's lack of enthusiasm over being made a grandmother and no longer wanting to follow her mother's house rules, my cousin left home. She and her baby bounced from place to place, staying until they had worn out their welcome. My cousin approached my mother to ask if she could live in our house. Ma was willing to watch the baby for a while, but she was highly disappointed in my cousin. My cousin—now deceased—was Ma's favorite niece, and she had expected better of her. Ma berated my cousin for getting pregnant without being married and for bringing another child into my aunt's house—already crowded with kids— and lashed out at her for not completing her high school education. Seeing that she wasn't going to elicit any sympathy out of Ma, my cousin moved on to find another relative or friend who might make room for her and her baby.

Much later in the evening, after Ma's temper had cooled down, I told her that I would never show up with a baby and no husband attached. It was then I realized that my mother hadn't been joking about what she'd do if I had an unplanned pregnancy. As I moved through my teen years, I paid close attention to the girls who had "gotten caught," as Ma put it. Their lives seemed to stop and stagnate once they learned the pregnancy test was positive, yet they'd still brag about "my baby this" and "my baby that." The girls continued to brag as even more kids came along that they couldn't deal with any better than the first. I had goals, and having a baby would seriously hinder me from reaching them. I never stopped having goals, and those goals never mixed with or included having children, so I opted to remain childless. What I wanted to do always seemed more interesting than babysitting for eighteen to twenty-one years.

Fifties Plus

Noriko Shibata, 51
Homemaker
Tokyo, Japan

When I was too young, I liked reading family stories like *What Katy did*, or *Little Women*. Having only one brother, I used to imagine how fun it would be to have sisters and brothers. I expected to be a mother with two or three children.

My aunts and uncles on my father's side are all parents, but I have a childless aunt on my mother's side. She was good at sewing and made my clothes. As she was a quiet person, talking with her was not always easy. But I never thought she was strange or weird or immature because of being childless.

My mother sometimes said, "Childless people are strange and immature," and added, "Don't be like your aunt."

I would challenge her. "Why are they strange," I would say, "because they didn't have children? *That's* strange!"

I married a thirty-four-year-old engineer in 1986. One year later, my mother and his parents began to ask, "When are you going to start a family?" and "Why don't you go see a doctor?" They wanted me to have a baby as soon as possible.

Both of us wanted a baby, but we were infertile. Our parents really wanted a grandchild. "Not yet pregnant? Why don't you try another doctor? Try another treatment." We got tired of all the pressure and began to think about living without children.

We decided to stop the infertility treatments in 1995. Our decision wasn't accepted by our parents. We didn't try to persuade them. So began our childfree life.

When I decided not to have a child sixteen years ago, I felt isolated in this child-friendly world. Now I have many friends with no children. I also enjoy exchanging messages with my schoolmates who have children. "Why didn't you have children?" they say. "When you get elderly, you will be lonely. Adopt a child."

None of my close friends talk like that.

Childfree living is good for me. I like my lifestyle, and I'm proud of my childfree life.

Marlene Gale, 52
Medical Assistant

Ft. Lauderdale, Florida

I am the youngest of four girls, and only one of my sisters chose to have children. Our mom died when I was ten, and my sisters were twelve, sixteen and eighteen, respectively. Most people think that our mother's death is the reason the three of us didn't have children. Maybe that is somewhat true, but I remember at age eight saying I did not want kids. I believe that I instinctively sensed the burden and struggle involved.

I have noticed that for many men it is a turn-off. I know that sounds awful, but marriages often end as a result of having children. Today, men are always shocked but almost always thrilled when I say I do not want children.

I would not have been a good mother; I realized that a long time ago. I enjoy older children but have never cared to be around infants, toddlers or small children. Mothers are very special people. I am thankful that my friends' mothers became mine.

Honestly, I just knew I did not have what it takes to do that job.

Anonymous, 53
Medical Secretary

Seattle, WA

For as long as I can remember, I've known I did not want children. I've never heard my biological clock ticking. I didn't see babies and long to have one. Now that I'm past menopause, I don't feel as if I'm "less of a woman" because my ability to make babies is gone. I've never tied my femininity to the ability to reproduce. Maybe I'm not genetically hardwired for the task. So is it nature or nurture, or a little of both? Some might say that being raised in a dysfunctional household (divorced parents, living with a single mother with an alcohol problem) and not having a solid "mother role model" could be a "cause" (as if I had a disease or something!) but I also had a loving stepmother providing an example of what a good mother could be. And I don't dislike kids; I just never wanted one of my own. I have never, for one single moment, regretted my choice to remain childless.

Some people are born to be mothers and do it amazingly, but I've also known others who never should have attempted parenthood. And surprisingly, I've heard people admit that if they had the chance to do it all again, they never would have had children. From what I've observed, a lot of men would be perfectly happy without children, but they do it to please their wives/partners. Not everyone is cut out for it, and that's not a bad thing. What's bad is when you don't acknowledge that fact and do it anyway, bringing misery to a lot of lives.

Life doesn't just happen. We have choices and should take responsibility for them. Having a child is a choice. Too many people become parents with no forethought, because "That's just what you do when you get married," or they didn't have a solid plan for birth control, or they thought a baby would hold their relationship together or give them the love they're missing. They don't seem to have developed any sort of life plan that extends beyond today. They don't realize how major this decision is, that it will affect everything they do for the rest of their lives, not to mention their children's lives.

My husband and I have made careful choices. The result is the happiness and security we have today. We chose educational and career pursuits that fulfilled us. Now, in our fifties, neither of us needs to work for financial reasons—partly because we didn't have to spend our money on child-rearing. We don't live extravagantly or own a lot of "things," because that's not who we are, but we don't deny ourselves, either. Our home is a quiet sanctuary where we enjoy spending time. We pursue our shared and independent personal interests. We give back to our community in a variety of ways. And most importantly, we make each other our priority and have a strong, loving relationship (after nearly twenty-eight years together, twenty-three of them married). This is how we've chosen to live our lives, and we're glad we did.

Amy, 54

Veterinary Clinic Manager

Novato, California

When I was in my teens, we visited family friends who didn't have kids. Instead, they had two little dogs they adored. They had a really nice life and a great house with a view of Puget Sound. They seemed really happy—no yelling or drama. I wanted to be just like them.

Like most teenage girls, I babysat for friends. My older sister really had fun with the kids she babysat, playing games, etc. I preferred to play with their pets. It's not that I have no motherly instincts; my pets are a huge part of my family. In fact, our lives revolve around them.

People tell me all the time I should have had children because I am such a good dog and cat mom. Now that I am an adult, I enjoy playing with my friends' children ... as long as they are well behaved.

I always assumed I'd have kids because that's what you do, right? But I never got around to it in my five-year marriage. In my current relationship of twenty-six years, my significant other never wanted kids. We were fine with our cats and dogs (along the line we acquired a cockatiel and a hamster). It's just as well because my husband survived cancer at forty-seven and a heart attack at fifty-four. He only has time to take care of himself; he lives in pain and struggles daily. He feeds our dogs and takes them outside to relieve themselves, but I do everything else. Hard to imagine taking care of kids, though by now they'd be adults.

I do wonder what it would be like to have grown kids ... and what will happen to me when I am old and alone. But, that's not a reason. I never wondered about having little kids when I was a young adult. People say it's never the right moment—not enough money, not enough time ... I had not enough interest.

Catherine Treadgold, 54

Publisher/Classical Singer

Seattle, Washington

From the time I first became mentally aware (age three), I began to receive mixed messages from my fiercely intelligent but traditional mother. She had been "first" in her law school class, but they gave the award to a man because she would "just get married and never practice." Which is exactly what she did. She met and married my father shortly after receiving her law degree and passing the Bar, and they took off for Oxford, where my father was a Rhodes Scholar. She immediately became pregnant with my brother and never practiced law.

So the message I received as a child was, "Get all your advanced degrees but never use them." My father spent a lot of time at work; he was professor of Russian History and in off-hours enjoyed nothing more than working on his research. He was a loving man, but typical of fathers in those days—not around a lot. He adored little children but didn't know what to do with the burgeoning adult. I realized early on that he was more comfortable around his students. My mother had too much energy to concentrate wholly on being a housewife, and I could tell that she often felt neglected by my father. She took on many volunteer activities, one of which turned into a full-time position. At the age of fifty, she re-entered the work force and later became a powerful, successful, and well-respected businesswoman (Harvard had once tried to recruit her into a business master's program—another opportunity she gave up to marry my father). She even passed the Bar Exam in Washington State, just in case. Although my mother changed her tune in midlife, the old one continued to play in my head.

Although I concentrated on academics (we all did; it was difficult not to in a family like mine), I vowed that someday I'd make creative fulfillment and fun my priorities (which didn't work out entirely as I planned, but that's another story). At Princeton I majored in German Literature. My goal was to become an opera singer, and German seemed to be the only major with any relevance. (I tried studying music, but the program emphasized composition, and I had zero talent at that.) Most opera libretti are pulp material—poorly written and based on popular dramas of the time. But I had discovered the work of respected Austrian writer Hugo von Hofmannsthal, who corroborated with Richard Strauss on one of my favorite operas, *Der Rosenkavalier* (The Rose Bearer). At Princeton we were required to write both Junior Papers and a Senior Thesis, so I chose the libretto of Hofmannsthal's *Die Frau ohne Schatten* (The Woman Without a Shadow) as the subject of my Junior Paper. I had never seen the opera and had no idea what it was about; I just trusted that if Hofmannsthal had written it, it would be interesting.

The Woman Without a Shadow is a complicated fairy tale opera about an Emperor who captures a gazelle who turns into a woman who can't bear children because she used to be a gazelle ... anyway, she has no shadow, and she convinces an ordinary woman—The Dyer's Wife—to give over her shadow. The Dyer's Wife doesn't want children and is fine with exchanging her shadow for riches and a handsome lover, thus putting her soul in jeopardy. The Unborn Children sing in an offstage chorus, urging their mother to give them life. The Dyer is so angry with his shadowless wife that he almost kills her, thus tainting the shadow, which is now unacceptable to the Empress. In German literature, the shadow is a symbol of the soul—in this case also immortality, which the Dyer's wife is denying both herself and her husband.

In the end, after a lot of rigmarole, the Empress gets her own shadow, the Dyer's Wife gets her shadow back, and the Unborn Children rejoice. This intensely irritating theme got me thinking about the whole issue of children and immortality. I always assumed I'd have children, even though I had never played with baby dolls or fantasized about motherhood. I wanted a career, freedom, fun. I didn't want drudgery, and I didn't even want marriage. I had never perceived my parents' marriage as particularly fulfilling for either of them, although they did become great companions in later life. It seemed that my mother gave up everything for a man who didn't appreciate her sacrifice. (If my mother were still alive, she'd surely argue otherwise.) After college I dated a lot of "inappropriate" men—none of whom had any interest in marriage. Because all my relationships had pull-dates, I was never tempted to give up my "brilliant" career. Whenever a man became serious about commitment, he made it clear he expected me not to travel; touring (I was doing musical theater at the time) would have been out of the question. Needless to say, I ran. These were actors, singers, conductors—men who would have screamed if I'd asked the same of them. They also had the old, tired melodies playing in their heads.

I have been with Jeff for five years. He has grown children, and fortunately they and their partners are terrific people. I sometimes wonder if I did the right thing by not having children (my brother and sister did not have their own families, either), because we did get some extraordinary genetic gifts. However, I see evidence that both the Treadgold and the Granquist branches have carried on our best traits and talents, and there are a few genes—mental illness, depression—that I hope will be lost to the gene pool.

Do children really make us "immortal"? The children of most of my friends hardly resemble them at all, and if they inherited their talents, they didn't inherit their dreams. Expecting immortality from one's children is a recipe for disappointment. They say your grandchildren resemble you most, but most of my friends waited until the eleventh hour—when they were already forty or older—so will they get to enjoy their grandchildren? Who even remembers their great-grandparents, except as faces in photographs?

I spent several years as an adjunct professor of voice at a community college and teaching kids of all ages at home. I enjoyed many of the children and young adults and always looked forward to seeing the enthusiastic *and* talented ones—about two percent of my studio. I might have relished motherhood if I'd had a chance to raise one of them. But what are the odds? It's not as though we are allowed to hand-pick our children's genetic makeup.

If I *had* become a mother, I would have loved my children no matter what. But who knows how I would have raised them? I would have made mistakes, too—probably different ones than my mother's. These are different times.

Ruby Hansen Murray, 58

Writer and Photographer
Puget Island, Washington

When I was young, I didn't want to be a mother, I wanted to be a writer.

The definition of "family" to me was "hypersensitive people shut up together in a box. "

I remember when we were traveling across country in the early-seventies. I was almost twenty, my brother a teenager, Jennie and John in middle school. We left a motel for dinner, driving in the blue Monte Carlo.

Choosing a restaurant was so difficult, it was painful. Let me out of this car.

I'm in fifth grade with my father at the mall in El Paso after school. I can't find him at the time we're supposed to meet. "Where *were* you? I'm never going with you again," he says and means it.

I kept a bracelet he bought me for a school dance. He had a round-cheeked pride that left a sentimental wash of good feeling.

My mother lies on my bed in the twilight of a summer evening. I'm under a sheet, she's stretched out singing "You always hurt the one you love..." a sweet-sort of apology in her voice. Her attention a luxury undercut by Jim Beam.

Those were the nights I lay with a rosary, praying that the battles over the light switch, the air conditioner thermostat would be averted. Those nights killed any belief in prayer.

In the '70s there were no women authors on literature lists and no indication there should be.

I couldn't imagine getting married and living the life of my boyfriend's family. They were conservative golf people, raw-boned and content. I would have become an alcoholic.

I might have pretended that I could find a way to write and have a child, if I had a partner. But I couldn't bear to inflict how irritable I am on someone else. I couldn't bear to feel the love, the smothering pride for a child, my own flesh.

When I see a writer acquaintance with dull-brown hair, a business skirt on her barrel-round body, sitting in a restaurant with her awkward son, I can imagine it even less. Too frightening to offer only myself to a child as a model of how to be in the world.

Brenda Brody, 61
College English Teacher
Chicago, Illinois

I remember that it was a nice day. My boyfriend and I were sitting on the couch watching TV, and we had plans to go out with friends later that night. I think we were watching a movie when I felt it—that sudden wrenching cramp that announced I was ovulating. Mittelschmerz, it's called. Though most women don't actually feel it, I always did. I must have yelped or made some sign because my boyfriend looked at me and asked what was wrong.

"I'm ovulating," I told him.

"You can tell?" he asked. I explained it to him and settled back against his big muscular chest. He sat still, however, and gazed at me.

"What?" I asked.

"Let's make a baby," he said breathlessly, a slight leer in his eyes.

"Let's not and say we did," I replied, but he wasn't deterred.

We had been dating for several months and had had good times. I was in graduate school and he was a freshman. I was also teaching classes so it was lucky he wasn't one of my students.

He sat up straight and looked at me and said, "I think we should make a baby. We're in love and we make a good couple. We're planning on moving when you graduate and I think we'd make a beautiful baby."

We were very different. He was a big muscular blonde with deep blue eyes and a boyish grin. I am a short black woman. We had heard numerous comments about how pretty a baby we would make. And, although it wasn't obvious visually, there was a considerable age difference. I was well aware that this was one of those on campus relationships that would not last past the next semester because I was graduating and he wasn't.

"I don't want to graduate pregnant and then have to move and look for a job," I told him. "This is really not the right time for this."

"It's never the right time," he argued, "people always say that, but they always find a way. You can get public aid if you don't have a job but I can find a job and hold things down till you are able to go to work."

What a knucklehead, I thought.

"That will never happen. And you have to finish school if you go with me, just like we discussed."

I realized then I was going to have to drop some reality on him. He wasn't thinking this through and the truth was I didn't want to have a baby at all, and really not with his immature butt. This man was fun to play with and all but he was not husband or father material. What kind of idiot would I be to get pregnant then and there with that man? I suddenly knew I didn't want to have a baby *at all, ever.*

For the next few minutes I spoke from my heart. I said all those things that I had been thinking that needed to be said. He did not argue or tell me that he would stay with me no matter what. He did not say he would take any kind of job and work as hard as he had to in order to support us. He didn't say any of those things that a woman wants the man in her life to say. I knew then that we would not be together much longer.

He reached inside my shirt and tried to squeeze my breast in an attempt to initiate lovemaking, hoping I would get so carried away that I would forget. "We can talk about it later," he whispered, between kisses.

I pulled away and stood up.

"No," I said, "we won't talk about this again. I don't want to have a baby with you now or ever. I don't want to have a baby at all with anyone."

I went to find something for the cramping. And the headache that had crept up the back of my neck as I saw the look on his face.

We broke up a few weeks later. It was the right thing to do.

Authors/Editor
Discussion

Coffeetown's publisher, Catherine Treadgold, who is childless, met us for lunch to discuss the essays received from around the world. Below is the transcript of our discussion.

Patricia: After reviewing each of the essays received, I made a list of sentences or phrases that popped out at me. One of the stories discussed how the author was "raised in an abusive home, and that she didn't think she could be a better parent than her own parents were." I thought it was interesting that she chose not to procreate because she felt she might be an abusive parent as well. Did you interpret it that way?

Catherine: Yes, I remember that ... and actually I can relate—not to the abusive part. My parents were not at all abusive, but my mother was such an over-achiever and so ambitious for us that the pressure was intense. She seemed to want to live vicariously through us, because she had given up so much to raise us. If I had my own children, I'd be worried they would make specific choices just to please me.

Patricia: Yes exactly .... My mother was a very good mother, a very motherly type. As a child I observed that a lot of the caretaker responsibilities were placed on her, as they were for most mothers back in the day. Father would come home from work and sit down at the dinner table while mother catered to his every need. It's the type of thing you would see on TV shows in the fifties.

Catherine: Yes, it was expected of that generation.

Patricia: Of course I never visited my father at his job to see how hard he worked, so I was clearly only seeing one side of the story. But, to my young eyes, Father had the power, the money, the freedom ... and Mother was the caretaker. I thought to myself, I want to be like Dad! I loved my mother and appreciated all she did and sacrificed for us, but I preferred my father's role. I never expressed any of this to my mother, because I didn't want her to feel that I didn't respect her. The roles just didn't seem to weigh evenly to me.

Catherine: I was upset by the way the men in my family seemed to be coddled. When I complained, Mom would say, "Don't argue, it's just the way it is. They do their part, don't worry about them, you just take care of things." And I would just think, *Mom, you have this advanced degree ... why are you the one doing everything?*

Renee: Exactly, just because she is a female.

Patricia: I think women still embrace that "Superwoman" role, trying to do everything. Of course it was expected of them then. It still is, in many cases.

Catherine: They had ways of getting what they wanted. My mother would say, "I'm working on him." I think a lot of women were good at that in those days.

Janice: She really said that?

Catherine: Yes, she finally got my father to quit smoking after "working on" him for about sixteen years. But there was a problem with that: I knew she was "working on" me, too. She was an excellent manager. After she went back into the workforce she managed paralegals for a law firm, instead of practicing law. I think she'd have been happier if she'd worked while we were growing up. I felt bad for her ... she could have been a judge.

Patricia: I always believed that my mother wanted to do more with her life, although she never admitted as much to my brother and me. But once, when my husband and I had gone out to dinner with her, I learned more. When I returned from the ladies' room, she was in the middle of telling Eric that her life's dream was to own an Arthur Murray Dance Studio. In her youth she had worked as an interior designer and used a lot of her hard-earned money studying dance at Author Murray. I thought to myself, why is she telling him this? I never heard this story. But then I realized that this was a dream, a yearning that had existed deep inside her. Did she regret never pursuing her dream?

Janice: Wow ... interesting.

Patricia: Personally, I have never felt maternal. There were several essays that said the same thing. However, I do feel maternal towards my dog. When my dad or my husband watch me with her, they say, "You would have made a great mom." I usually respond, "Yes, I know, but I prefer this."

Renee: Yes, I feel that way about my cat.

Janice: Did you notice in how many of the stories, affections went from babies to animals?

Renee: Fur-kids!

Catherine: Fur-children.

Janice: Yeah, absolutely!

Catherine: I had never heard that expression before reading these stories.

Janice: These are all nurturing people, but they nurture animals ... not people. At least, not children. And that's, like, my whole family! All of us have animals, dogs and birds.

Patricia: I found stories that began with, "I'm an only child" intriguing, since I'm *not* an only child. We received quite a few like that. I always thought kids who were only children learned to entertain themselves, because they have nobody to interact with outside of their parents. You grow up less dependent on others for entertainment or what not. You develop more interests and find ways to amuse yourself. I think "only children" probably grow up to become better prepared to handle the senior citizen phase, because they know how to be alone.

Renee: I never thought of that, but it really makes sense.

Patricia: Even though I have a brother, we both had different interests. I lean heavily toward the creative side, and creative endeavors are typically done alone.

Catherine: Did you all do a lot of babysitting?

Janice: Absolutely. As a first-born, I had the responsibility of babysitting my brother and sister at a really early age. So instead of being their sibling friend, I became their authority figure. In a lot of the essays the women were caretakers of their siblings, or they babysat the neighbors' kids and saw how incompetent they were as parents.

Patricia: I babysat between the ages of twelve and eighteen years. There was a lot of opportunity, because the military community was tight-knit. Everybody knew everybody. When I became older, and my father retired from the military, I had an opportunity to work as a full-time nanny to two little girls who were still in diapers, and I handled them just fine. They were not in a good situation. Most of the time they had nothing in the fridge but beer and leftovers, and I would have to call my mom to bring over milk, bread, peanut butter and jelly. I felt really bad for the girls, but continued to do the job I'd agreed to do. I was surprised how attached I became to the girls at the end, knowing the situation I would be leaving them in. The youngest girl even started to call me Mommy. When I went back to pick up my paycheck, the parents and the two little girls had jumped ship. They hadn't paid their lease that month, and they never paid me. I was upset for myself, but more upset for those two little girls. I still wonder what happened to them.

Renee: They were lucky to have you with them that summer.

Patricia: I didn't mind babysitting that age group. But, I wasn't fond of the terrible twos and older. Although I did a tremendous amount of babysitting in my youth and always felt I was able to handle kids just fine, today they exhaust me. Perhaps it has something to do with the years of dedication to work and school, having established a habit of coming and going as I please. If I'm around kids for more than a couple of hours, I really start to feel drained. Ironically, I don't feel that way around my dog.

Catherine: I had some really bad babysitting experiences, because I didn't know what I was doing and nobody explained anything. I didn't even know how to put a diaper on. This one couple was desperate for a babysitter and didn't ask about my experience, but I must have been around twelve. The baby screamed and screamed and screamed, until I began crying. So I called my mother and she came over. My mother said, "The baby can sense your tension!"

I said, "Yes, I'm tense all right!"

(Everyone laughs.)

Catherine: I thought, "Oh my God, how do people put up with this?"

Patricia: In contrast to the only-child's viewpoint, there were those people who grew up in households with too many kids. One contributor states, "I am the youngest of twelve. There were too many kids, too limited resources, not enough beds, clothes, food, or love to go around." I found her story interesting because as the youngest, she was an observer of her environment and seem to figure out early on what she wanted. She went on to be the only one of twelve kids to receive her college degree, to establish a successful business on her own. That essay was the perfect example of childhood experiences influencing decisions made later in life, in this case, deciding not to have children, pursuing an education, and building a lucrative career.

Catherine: Do you remember the essay—I think it was from France—where the person said the more children you have the more the government will pay for them? She really resented that because she didn't have the opportunities that children with multiple siblings enjoyed.

Janice: Yes, that's right. The government would give scholarships to children with multiple siblings, but because she didn't have a lot of siblings, she had to put herself through school.

Patricia: Renee, when you lived in Dukar or Senegal, did they offer women with children that same opportunities?

Renee: There really is no incentive—other than social or cultural—to have children. Their culture and their religion encourage it. The government isn't directly responsible. I think it would be beneficial for the government to promote independence and education. In these developing nations, there is a lot of incentive for people to go to school, even though they don't necessarily respond.

Catherine: In Europe many people—especially men—died in World War I and II. So the government became very pro-child, offering all sorts of incentives.

Janice: Look at Vietnam! Wow, practically a whole generation gone!

Catherine: In Africa, if you can decrease the infant mortality rate then people will stop having so many children. Two generations ago people had tons of kids because so many of them died. Out of ten, maybe two would survive.

Janice: When I talk about Vietnam, I mean the Vietnamese, not us. A whole lot more of them were killed than Americans.

In the same vein, back to talking about the oldest child ... A lot of the stories concerned how the parents handled parenthood. Perhaps they didn't have enough time, were overworked, etc. That's where my decision came from, observing my mother when she was young and how she handled three tiny ones. I was the oldest. In my tiny little mind, I thought, That's not going to be me.

Renee: Wow ... you were already thinking like that at such an early age?

Janice: Yes, and I had no idea where that came from, because I *like* kids, but observing my parents had a huge impact.

Catherine: Fathers were treated like Kings, and sons like Princes.

Patricia: I guess I wanted to be a King instead of a Queen.

(Laughter.)

Catherine: There was that great sense of injustice. Like I felt toward my brother ... I'm no different from you, why should I have to make your sandwich? My mother didn't do him any favors, because eventually he had to make his own sandwiches. I know how to cook!

Janice: Yes, that's really not preparing your son for marriage. When I raised my stepson, Gavin, I wanted to raise him so he would be a good husband and father. I didn't want him thinking a woman was going to be what we had to be—subservient to his needs. A lot of mothers don't think about that when they raise sons.

Catherine: My boyfriend cooks. He's lived alone for a very long time so he's completely independent. He'll come over to my house and fix things just because they bug him. He has great handyman instincts, which I lack because I was raised to cook and clean ... what a women was taught to do.

Patricia: Yes, my husband was very self-sufficient before we got married. He was thirty. He had time to live on his own and learn to do everything himself. I love how neat and clean he is. But he didn't cook when he was younger, and today he still does not cook. Fortunately that is something I love doing.

One of the phrases I read in one of the essays really bothers me whenever I hear it: "People who choose not to have children are missing out." The sentence never seems to finish. What are we missing out on? If it's such a great thing, you should be able to put it into words.

Janice: They typically follow that up with, "Oh, we can't describe it; you have to experience it to really understand."

Renee: An article or study came out recently that proves that people who have children are noticeably less happy on average. Have you heard this? There are some people with children who are exuberantly happy, but others who are not. On average your level of happiness decreases after that first child.

Patricia: I heard something similar on Dr. Phil a few years back. He sponsored an anonymous survey of married couples across the United States. A large percentage stated if they could do it over, they would not have children; the lifestyle was simply too stressful. And that was several years back. Imagine how parents today feel, trying to raise kids with all the distractions available to them these days.

Catherine: A lot of the authors in the essays said they didn't feel they got the attention they needed. Some also admitted that maybe they, as children, required too much attention. They didn't want a child they couldn't give enough attention to. So it's kind of strange. They were saying "Okay, I didn't get what I needed in my youth, but I don't blame my parents because I couldn't give a child that, either. And I don't think you should have a child unless you are willing to give it that kind of attention." I kind of agree with that. I think too many people who have children farm out the responsibilities to others.

Renee: Exactly, it's a different experience.

Catherine: I have a friend who was raised by a Nanny, and her Nanny meant more to her than her own mother.

Patricia: It's like that book, *The Help*.

All: Oh yeah … that was such a good movie, too. And such a good indication of how children were, and still are, raised by folks with money. Great movie.

Patricia: Another phrase in one of the essays especially touched me: "When people find out I do not have any desire to have kids, I'm viewed as some kind of oddity. People just assume there must be something wrong with me."

I remember one incident in my cubical community. That day several women were going out to lunch, but I had to pass because I needed to get caught up on school work. After they came back from lunch, I asked one of the women, "How was lunch?" She said, "Fine." Then she stared at me for a second and added, "There's nothing wrong with you, just because you didn't have kids." She put her purse in her desk and walked away.

Catherine: They'd been talking about you.

Janice: Oh my!

Patricia: I thought, Thank you for telling me that. Now I know I'm the topic of discussion. Here we go again!

Catherine: Have your friends with kids ever said, "If I could turn back the clock I probably would not have children. I love my children, but I would not do it again"?

Janice: Yes, I've heard that many times!

Renee: I've heard exactly the opposite. They say, "If I had to do it all over again I would do it exactly the same way. My children mean everything to me."

Catherine: Yeah, but sometimes they are talking to themselves.

(Laughter.)

Renee: So true. They are trying to convince themselves that they made the right decision. Nobody wants to think they made the wrong decision.

Catherine: One of my neighbors who just had a baby told me, "You know, it's a lot more work that you think it's going to be." She had this notion that once she had a child she'd have more in common with her friend who was also a mother. They could all get a babysitter and do things together as a family. But it's turned out to be a lot more than she bargained for.

Patricia: Do you feel there is still as much pressure for women to have children as in the past?

Catherine: Oh my gosh, yes.

Patricia: I mean, now that women have evolved to the point where many are educated and have careers, you would think the pressure to have kids on top of all that would subside.

Catherine: I don't think it has subsided anywhere. It's interesting, when you read about countries like Sweden, Finland, and other places there is still pressure. Perhaps not as much as in the U.S., though.

Patricia: One Russian women says she has to work three jobs just to support herself. She implied that, if money were no object, she'd want to be married and have a child

Renee: Yes, I have heard Russian women do not have as many children.

Catherine: The Russian men don't want to get married and have children because of economic conditions.

Patricia: Men do not want to take on the burden of caring for both a woman and a child. I have a Russian friend who confirmed that it is hard to find a Russian man who can provide for his family. She finally moved to America and married an American man who was willing to have a child even though it was late in life for both. She was forty-eight when she gave birth. They used in vitro.

Catherine: I have several actor/singer friends who, after they reached the point in their lives when they knew their careers were not going to take off, decided to have children. It was like, okay, I didn't have the career I wanted, so now it's time to have a child, something to validate my existence. One friend finally got pregnant in her forties, after many fertility treatments. Before she finally conceived, at every family function her relatives would ask, "So when are you going to have a baby?" until she was convinced that her happiness depended on it.

Janice: This reminds me of that creative process essay. How nurturing is a form of the creative process. The woman in that essay just wants to create in her business or the arts in lieu of creation by procreation. Both are still creating, just in different forms.

Patricia: There is so much truth in that. If I had a kid I would not be able to do a lot of the things that bring me pleasure in life. I know myself; if I'd had a kid, I would have devoted all my time and energy into making sure the kid was raised right, instead of bettering my career, furthering my education, pursuing my passions. I was afraid of having a kid and later feeling like I missed out in life. So far, no regrets.

Catherine: In one essay the woman mentioned visiting childless family friends who always seemed happy and fulfilled and fun-loving. That couple were her positive role models: they had no kids, but they had dogs. She ended up adopting that same lifestyle. Kids can have role models other than their parents—aunts, uncles, teachers and family friends can be just as inspirational in lieu of bad mothers, bad fathers, absent fathers, abusive parents, over-achieving parents. When I was growing up, my parents had some really cool single friends. Remember that movie, *Auntie Mame*? I used to think I was going to be Auntie Mame—the crazy, goofy, fun, positive-role-model Auntie.

Patricia: When I was young, I had an Aunt Mary who never married or had kids. I always thought she was a pleasant person to be around. Aunt Mary was the oldest of five, and her mother died young, so she took on the caretaker role. I often wonder if she didn't get married or have kids because she felt like she'd been there and done that. She ended up working in a department store and supporting herself.

Catherine: My Great-Aunt Blanche, whose wedding ring I wear, was the youngest of ten children. She was the loveliest person. My last grandfather died when I was about eight, and my last grandmother died the year I was born, so Auntie Blanche was the closest I ever had to a grandmother. She had the most wonderful sense of humor. I adored her. She married late and never had children. I think she just loved us. She was a positive role model for me.

If you know cool single people or happily married people who don't have kids, you don't have the same pressure to conform. As long as you can handle being the odd duck in the family.

Renee: People who don't get married have to constantly explain themselves as well. I have a cousin who never married, and all these years everybody was wondering why because he's such a handsome young guy. He's in his forties now and looks great. As it turns out, he was gay. He finally just came out after all these years.

Janice: I was struck by the essay where the women is the oldest of six, doesn't want a child of her own, but really wants the birthing experience.

Renee: That's unusual, all right.

Patricia: How many women want that?

Janice: Right! There was no surrogacy in the State of Washington so she never did it. But she wanted to give birth and then give the child to its original mother. She never wanted her own child, but now she has a stepdaughter. She followed the same path as I did, marrying a man with a child and becoming a stepmother.

Janice: Renee, how are you feeling about having children? When you tried before, you weren't able to conceive. But you are still young, and things could change. You could still try.

Renee: I'm not one hundred percent against having children, but I'm not one of those women who feel that they just have to have a child. It's just something I never really think about.

Janice: Do your parents ever talk to you about it?

Renee: You know, surprisingly, they don't want me to have a child.

Janice: What?

Renee: I will be completely honest with you. They told me they don't want me bringing a child into the world who is doomed to hell. Because they think if I have a child while living this kind of lifestyle—living with my boyfriend in lieu of marriage, not going to church, not adhering absolutely to Christian beliefs—then I'd be creating a life that is going to be continually tormented in hell.

Janice: Wow!

Renee: That's exactly what they told me. Although it's hurtful, at the same time it works out because they're not pressuring me. But because of that, there's part of me that's like, well now I want to have a kid because you feel that way!

(Laughter.)

Renee: So that's the way it is. And really, I don't believe in hell and just can't wrap my mind around that concept. There are so many humans who are tortured here on earth, so many places and situations that could already be considered hell.

Patricia: It can be both heaven and hell here on earth.

Renee: Yes. So my parents are not at all insisting I have a child. But if I broke up with my boyfriend and got in the perfect relationship with some Christian guy who met their standards, they would definitely be interested in me procreating.

Janice: Do they have grandchildren?

Renee: Yes, my brother has three children, and my parents are obsessed by them and visit them frequently. I feel sorry for my brother's family because they are tucked away in Eastern Oregon, isolated from everyone. None of their family lives nearby; it's just the two of them. My brother lives in California so they often travel there.

Janice: Is your brother living the type of life your parents would have wanted?

Renee: Yes, I think to some extent because the kids are being raised as Christians. The youngest just accepted Jesus into her heart, which was a big thing on Facebook the other day.

Patricia: Would you ever consider adoption?

Renee: Ummm, yes, possibly. If I was in the right circumstances— getting the education I want and financially secure. I'm working toward those two goals. But at the same time, I do enjoy the freedom of not having a child. I like to plot out my life and think maybe I want to go further and become a dermatologist. I currently have the time and flexibility to do that.

Patricia: I find that the longer you wait, the more you get used to your freedom and using that time to enjoy the things you love to do.

Renee: Yeah, and maybe five years from now I'll treasure my freedom even more. Of course, by then it will be more difficult to conceive a child.

Catherine: You read interviews about these authors who have children and still write from four to six a.m. every morning before the kids get up. Congratulations to those who can both have children and fulfill their dreams. I hope they have children who don't resent their parents later in life because they spent so much time on themselves. When you hear some people talk about their parents, you think, *That doesn't sound so bad.* But every adult who talks about her childhood is suddenly a kid again, recalling all the bad stuff that really wasn't so bad; the memories are still being filtered through the perspective of their younger selves. Even the best parents accumulate a litany of sins in their children's minds.

Patricia: My only concern about choosing not to have kids is the unknown ... the future. I'm trying to ensure that I have a great income so that when I get older I'll have the means to hire the best caretakers; there aren't going to be any kids to help out. And even if there were, there's no guarantee they would be there for me.

Renee: I've been thinking along those lines as well ... who's going to take care of me when I get older.

Patricia: I don't think so much about how there won't be children to visit when I'm in a senior home. I go to these senior homes to visit relatives, and I see many older people whose kids are not even there for holiday dinners. I try not to focus on that so much, try to live for today, but you do have to plan for the future. Not just financially. For instance, I take lots of photographs when I travel, photographs that mean something to me. When I'm a senior citizen I'd like to create an oil painting of each of those photos as a way of retaining those memories and projecting them onto a canvas.

Renee: I love that! I love how you have your life planned.

Patricia: I just want to make sure I don't get lonely or bored when I get older, as so many do. My husband may not be around; there are just no guarantees. I also have things that I want to accomplish, because accomplishments are important to me as well.

Renee: Yes, and you live longer when you have that mindset and are engaged in things around you, rather than just sitting there, depressed because you're nearing the end of life.

Janice: I think Patricia is a really good example of someone who actually plans her life and has goals, because you tend to reach your goals.

Patricia: I think goal setting was just instilled in me ... although I'm only a Monday through Friday goal-oriented person, I do enjoy my weekends.

Janice: One of the contributors said, "I was born without the burning desire to be a mother, I don't have a choice, I was born that way." It wasn't her goal.

Patricia: You need that burning desire. If you don't have it, you're better off not having children.

Renee: We all know people whose kids were completely unplanned. It was like, "Whoops!"

Catherine: When you go to professional school for singing or acting, the first thing they say to you is, "If you don't want to do this more than anything in the whole world, then don't do it." That doesn't deter anybody, of course, because nobody imagines that she is going to be the person—one of the ninety-nine-point-nine percent—who is going to fail, to not be able to make a living at her art. Everyone thinks she is going to be the one whose dreams come true. The ones who made it were the ones who approached their artistic professions practically, without the stars in their eyes.

Janice: Reality sets in, and they see that it's a lot harder and less fun than they ever imagined.

Catherine: The same should hold true for parenting. What if somebody has a child with Down Syndrome and has to take care of him for the rest of her life? There are those that can do it—even joyfully—but imagine the effort and selflessness involved. Or if you have a child who inherits Great-Great Uncle Joe's horse thief genes ... it just never occurs to you that you might be the one ending up with the nasty kid no one can socialize. Our society urges everybody to take this chance, no matter what their abilities. Even the person who hates children is supposed to have children.

Patricia: The media has a lot to do with that. I used to love to watch

Entertainment Tonight to get highlights on my favorite movies or TV shows. Now, it's all about impossibly young celebrities with baby bumps or somebody's stint in rehab. Who cares?!

Renee: Yeah, with all the attention the media pays to celebrity babies, more irresponsible people are going to want kids. The media promotes children as a positive move for everyone. Americans want to do what celebrities do, even if it means having kids.

Patricia: And remember, celebrities don't necessarily raise the kid themselves. They have the money to hire full-time nannies. Which brings me to the part of the book that I think all women need to be reminded about. Marriages do not always work. Many women spend most of their years raising children and not working. Then one day they find themselves alone, forced to support both themselves and their children for the next decade. Finally they reach retirement age, having planned on sharing their husband's social security, which they are eligible to do if they do not remarry. However, they will not get the same amount as their ex-husband— only half as much! As long as he is alive, you will only get half his social security. If a couple wants to have kids, and fathers want mothers to stay at home and raise them, the fathers should pay double social security. Not only would this protect the mother's future, it would make Americans rethink their choices.

Catherine: I have to wonder how many people are that farsighted!

Janice: If a couple could see that far ahead, the husband still wouldn't pay double social security; he would make the wife go to work *and* raise the family.

Patricia: It's up to the woman to stand up for herself and say "No." Government needs to find a way to level the playing field. Poverty rates for males and females are the same through childhood, but increase for women during their childbearing years and again in old age. The most destitute people in the U.S. are retired senior women. How many of them do you think were mothers?

Do you remember that commercial with the jingle "I can bring home the bacon, fry it up in a pan, and never ever let you forget you're a man … because I'm a woman …". Who came up with that superwoman mentality?

Renee: I will say, though, that I grew up in a setting where my dad did a lot. He didn't do a lot of the housework, but he was always working, mowing the lawn, cleaning things up. He didn't just come home and sit down. So I have to give him more credit, even though he did more male-type duties. He was never one to sit down and say, okay, I'm going to watch the game now.

Catherine: My father was a professor so he had to publish in order to go forward in his profession. He often did his research at night … so I understand that. But Mother made it possible for him to have the time to excel in his career. Fortunately for her, she still had the genius to find her way back into the working world even after twenty years removed from the workforce. And they stayed together. I've seen a lot of women make that same sacrifice and get screwed over. Part of why they do everything they can to please their men is to keep him from leaving. But even then there is no guarantee.

Patricia: Maybe that's it. Maybe that's why women try to do it all, because they don't want their men to leave.

Catherine: She would be lost without his financial support, so she tries to make herself essential to him, to make him feel as if he'd be lost without her.

Janice: In a lot of cases he would be.

Patricia: That's the motivation.

Catherine: Religion was often a factor for these women.

Renee: Yes, usually in a negative context.

Catherine: Conservative religious families—whether they are Christian, Jewish, Muslim, whatever—expect you to obey your husband, be subservient to their needs, be fruitful and multiply.

Janice: Yes, what about the woman who was a Jehovah's Witness? Her father, who really had not wanted children, wouldn't let her have a blood transfusion. She would have died if her grandmother hadn't interceded.

Catherine: And she has no relationship with him anymore.

Janice: Right.

Patricia: Have you heard that old saying that people who don't have children have had unhappy childhoods?

Catherine: It contains an element of truth, and yet a lot of these essays refute it.

All: Agreed.

Catherine: One essay compares not wanting children to being homosexual, in that it is something we are often aware of quite early but wish to keep a secret.

Janice: That wasn't me! I spouted it out since I was four or five years old … I did not want children and I did not want to get married. But that's the type of kid I was. I was surprised when Patricia told me about her experiences in the corporate world, that she was looked upon as an oddity. I was still announcing that I didn't want kids when I was married and in my early twenties. But then, shortly thereafter, my stepson entered my life.

Patricia: Yes, and as long as I've known you, you've had a stepson. So from that point on, if the subject of kids came up, you would always talk about "my son" this, or "my son" that. You never carried the "I'm Not Procreating" sign like I did. This is when the stigma began for me, when in my late twenties I told people it was my choice. I had no stepchild to hide my choice behind. It was the large pink elephant in the room and still is.

Janice: Yes, in my youth, when I did announce it, I would always be told, "Oh you'll change your mind, you're still young."

Catherine: Yes, and that's the reason doctors are reluctant to perform tubal ligations or vasectomies on the young. People do change their minds. I do wonder if in some cases they finally agree to bear children because they fall in love with someone who really wants them.

Patricia: I think a lot of them also change their minds as a last resort to keep the marriage together, or because they get lonely, and they think kids are the antidote to loneliness.

Catherine: Yes, and that goes back to my friends who didn't fulfill their initial dreams; their dreams died so they tried to make up for it by having a child.

Janice: That creative thing again.

Catherine: Yes, they're like, "Here's something I can do that society will applaud. Now that I have a child, everyone will forget that I failed as an actress."

Patricia: I told my masseuse about this book and she completely understood the disapproval I face for not having kids. She feels that society disapproves of her for having only one child. She is constantly being asked, when are you going to have another?

Catherine: That's because she only hangs around with other parents.

Janice: Wow. Of course ... only one child. How will you think that will affect your child ... yada, yada, yada.

Patricia: This year the earth reached a population of seven billion. A couple of essays mentioned that.

Janice: How about the Asian-American woman who was the caretaker of her siblings. She mentioned that in the Asian community, she didn't feel the pressure to have children because education and career came first. She ended up getting a tubal ligation because she had already raised her younger siblings. She preferred having dogs over kids.

Patricia: A lot of animal lovers.

Catherine: Well, animals are loyal and trusting and you can pretty much figure out their personalities when you get them.

Patricia: Any more essays that stood out for anyone?

Catherine: There was the one women who said, "Infertility can be a curse if you let it be. For me, infertility has made me stronger and more adventurous." She's making lemonade from lemons.

Janice: Yes, she wanted a child, couldn't have a child, and then embraced it.

Catherine: Right, she embraced it. In general, I think it's your reaction to things that's more important than what actually happens. Because although a lot of people were childless by choice, there were several others who didn't make conscious choices. But they claimed their lives were richer for not having children; they allowed it to become a positive thing. In some cases it really was in their genes; they were just not maternal. And I don't know what makes you maternal ... does anyone? They say that at certain times in your hormonal cycle you're more maternal than others. Maybe it's all about estrogen. Perhaps if you have a child the hormonal thing kicks in even if you thought it wouldn't.

Patricia: I can see how once you've had a child, that has become your life now. So I can see how you have to take it on, you have to nurture it.

Janice: That's biological, because the human race had to survive. The mother had to protect the child, not just have the baby and say "See ya later." You had to fall in love with the child to protect it; that instinct originates with the beginning of the human race.

Patricia: Yes, it's nature versus nurture.

Janice: Like men having to spread their sperm around.

Catherine: Yes, I was reading about the biology of love not too long ago. Apparently sperm has a medicinal quality. Even if you don't have an orgasm, it is absorbed through your skin and enhances your mood.

Janice: Wow!

Renee: In some African countries they use sperm in some of their concoctions or remedies, like creams and such that you apply to your skin. But I didn't realize that it actually causes euphoria.

Patricia: Are you talking about testosterone?

Renee: Yes, that is it. It's suppose to make you feel better.

Catherine: It lifts your spirits.

Janice: Yes, that's also used when you enter menopause to help balance your testosterone levels. If you don't have a very good sexual desire, or libido, it will help increase that desire.

Catherine: Another essay mentioned a teacher who kept telling all her students, "If you get pregnant you're going to ruin your life." Mothers do that, of course.

Janice: Yes, they had the message pounded into their brains. Like the one mother who said, "If you get pregnant, you're out of the family," because she was so afraid of her daughter getting pregnant.

Catherine: Then there are those people who assume you are in poor health, and because of that you couldn't have a child, you couldn't get pregnant. That must be hard for people who are trying and can; they feel genetically inferior.

Patricia: Then there are those people who have "a list of things to do before they have kids." So they plan their lives to rush through these things they really want to do to get them out of the way before they have kids. They rush through life.

Janice: They're saying, there's no right time to have kids, because you can put it off and put it off, and before you know it, you're having problems conceiving because you waited too long.

Catherine: One said she had a wonderfully perfect childhood, that her mother sacrificed a lot to raise her. They were the popular family on the block; all the kids hung out with them. They were the coolest parents ever. However, she didn't feel like she owes her parents anything. I know my father was very disappointed that no one had children.

Janice: So was mine.

Patricia: I think my dad was a little disappointed that I didn't have kids, but he does have a couple of grandkids from my brother. That said, my mother didn't seem as disappointed.

Janice: My mom wasn't disappointed, either! She didn't seem to care one way or the other if we had grandchildren.

Patricia: Yeah, my mother was more concerned about me getting a good education and job.

Catherine: Some people seem to be crazy about babies, but don't really know what to do with them after that grow out of that cute stage.

Janice: That's funny because I really like babies but haven't had a chance to be around them much. But I will now that I have two grandchildren. I enjoyed Gavin growing up a lot, watching him go through different developmental stages since the age of seven. I liked the fact that when he got older he could understand more. I was better able to communicate with him.

Catherine: They don't stay in that darling baby stage for long. Any more essays to discuss?

Patricia: Those essays where people didn't feel maternal at all and never played with dolls.

Catherine: Yes, they preferred stuffed animals or other forms of entertainment in lieu of playing house with dolls. I don't know about you guys, but I never played a single game as a child that involved me having a child … no baby dolls for me.

Janice: I liked Barbie because she seemed independent. I think they had a career Barbie as well.

Patricia: I liked career Barbie and her Corvette, but my biggest fascination was the Easy Bake Oven, which really makes sense because I thoroughly enjoy cooking, I get lost in it. There's a correlation there.

Catherine: Yes, there are a number of things that seemed to be inborn.

Janice: Sometimes you don't really know if something is inborn because you are distracted by something else, like raising a child.

Renee: You might not even realize you have talents in other ways because your time is consumed by raising your child.

Patricia: One last thought: because I have chosen to pass on procreation, I have this strong need to give back. Perhaps that stems from being told I was selfish for making my decision, who knows? Part of me has adopted that view about myself, and I try to think of ways to give back in order to qualify my choice. Knowing I will never have a daughter, I do find myself wanting to help other young women by providing advice or tools to help them in life. It is my hope that through this book we can educate women through our experiences in hopes of making their choice an easier one. Perhaps our experiences will only be interesting to women who have chosen not to procreate or are contemplating whether or not to procreate. If anything, we can provide them with a number of perspectives. We don't know what influences this book will have on other women. My hope is they will feel positive about their choice, no matter what it will be.

We invite you to join the discussion.

If you have any questions for the authors,

you can find the Being Fruitful Without

Multiplying Group on Facebook.

Resources

Social Networking (Facebook)
Being Fruitful Without Multiplying Group
Childfree Chicks Group
Childfree Group
Childfree in a Natalist World Group
Childfree Mothers Connect
Childfree by Choice Group
Childfree Travel
Living Childfree with Pets Group
The Childless by Choice Project Group
The Childless Stepmom
The Childfree Life
No Kidding Worldwide Group
Stop Making Babies Group

Blogs and Websites
Being Fruitful Without Multiplying:
www.BeingFruitfulWithoutMultiplying.com/

Child Free Zone—Why More People Are Choosing Not
to Be Parents: www.childfree.com.au/

Childless by Marriage—
www.childlessbymarriage.blogspot.com

Gateway Women United Kingdom—www.Gateway-
women.com

Maybe Baby, Maybe Not—
www.MaybeBabyMaybeNot.com

No Children Please—www.NoChildrenPlease.com

Ramona Creel: What Childfree Means—
www.RamonaCreel.com

Reasons I Should Not Breed:
Acetonescribe.wordpress.com

The Childless by Choice Project:
www.ChildlessByChoiceProject.com

Books

Savvy Auntie: The Ultimate Guide for Cool Aunts, Great Aunts, Godmothers, and All Women Who Love Kids
Melanie Notkin (2011)

Complete Without Kids: An Insider's Guide to Childfree Living by Choice or by Chance
Ellen L. Walker. PhD (2011)

No Children, No Guilt
Sylvia D. Lucas (2011)

Two is Enough: A Couples guide to Living Childless by Choice - Kindle
Laura Scott (2009)

No Way Baby! Exploring, Understanding, and Defending the Decision NOT to Have Children
Karen Foster (2010)

I'm Taking My Eggs and Going Home: How One Woman Dared to Say No to Motherhood
Lisa Manterfield (2010)

Pride and Joy: The Lives and Passions of Women without Children
Terri Casey (2007)

50 Reasons Not to Have Kids: And What to Do If You Have Them Anyway
Joe Sindoni (2007)

Baby Not on Board
Jennifer L. Shawne (Chronicle Books, 2005)

Childfree and Loving It
Nicki Defago (Vision, 2005)

Questions for Book Clubs

Being Fruitful without Multiplying began as a conversation between three female relatives and then expanded into a dialog between women from many different countries and walks of life. In the Authors/Editor Discussion section, the three main authors discuss the essays from the other contributors. The following questions may help your own group begin its discussion.

1. When you finished reading this book, what was your general reaction?

2. Do you associate with certain social groups where you would feel uncomfortable discussing what you've read? What aspects of the book might be considered controversial or objectionable and why?

3. Did you feel that this book was fair to men?

4. How would your partner or friends react to this book?

5. Did this book give you new insights into your own decision to bear or not to bear children?

6. Did these stories give you a new understanding or sympathy for women who are childless or child-free by choice?

About the Authors

Patricia Yvette was raised an Air Force brat and so grew up in various locations abroad. She has a master's degree in E-Marketing Strategies, and is currently pursuing her PhD. Her career has been based in a Seattle aerospace company for the past twenty years. Married over twenty five years, she enjoys traveling, culinary art, outdoor recreation, and considers herself a life-long learner.

Renee Ann has served as a Christian missionary and traveled extensively through West Africa where she encountered an enlightening way of life. Life-challenging events altered her attitude toward the religion she was raised with and once advocated. She is now an aesthetician.

Janice Lynne has worked in the travel business for the past thirty-two years. She was Sales Director with a major cruise line for twenty-eight years and is currently Vice-President of Sales for a small boutique cruise line. She has been named Sales Person of the Year numerous times. Janice is a world traveler, stepmother, and published author of three children's books.

Made in the USA
Lexington, KY
16 November 2012